COSMIC MIND A GIFT OF LOVE

A JOURNEY OF SELF DISCOVERY THAT BEGINS WITH A HEARTFELT LETTER

NASEEM ANSARI

Made with ♥ on the Notion Press Platform
www.notionpress.com

Dedicated to:

My two loving daughters,

Lubna Faquih & Afreen Annis,

This book wouldn't have been possible without their ever presence in my thoughts.

Naseem Ansari

Business Address

This book is a work of non-fiction. Although the author and publisher have made every effort to ensure that the information in this book was correct at press time the author and publisher do not assume and hereby disclaim any liability for any loss, damage or disruption caused by error or omission whether such errors or omission result.

Contents

Contents

About The Author

Naseem Ansari
Business Address

This book is a work of non-fiction. Although the author and publisher have made every effort to ensure that the information in this book was correct at press time the author and publisher do not assume and hereby disclaim any liability for any loss, damage or disruption caused by error or omission whether such errors or omission result.

Acknowledgements

Divya Chauhan, a professional editor, who edited my book, observes:

I think the book's great..... While your book is well-researched, it does come across as a bit formal, almost like an academic paper. Your understanding of the world is evident and I appreciate that.

Deepika Kiron, a naturopath, and enthusiast of Vipassana meditation, for some inevitable, couldn't read beyond the 10th chapter. I am obliged to her for posting the comments she has read, verbatim:

"Read 1st chapter and am so overwhelmed.. while reading, I see as though. .. my thoughts hv been read by u. And you have penned it...."Am so excited to read   ur thoughts on spiritualism.".... "Freedom is wisdom if allowed with positive intentions and faith"..."It was a pleasure reading the 4th chapter.. *Tonic of Life* "Freedom, curiosity, fun, laughter,joy.. wow, wow, you hv done truly immense research too by giving references"..."How much of scientific research you have done on this topic and to mention the references also oh God I mean really I feel so excited"..."Nature cures. It's THE system, that knows how to work when we abide by nature's laws in terms of nutrition, and energy. Vibrations, frequency.   Well well said"..."I read Zygote   chapter and it's wonderful. How much of scientific research have you done on this topic".....read the chapter puzzle of life U hv made it simple I wonder how u researched and wrote with such simplicity"...." Emphasis on love, compassion,"..." Helps in healing, and is a powerful force for the smooth functioning of the universe, and cells at minute, energy levels."...Capitalism is truly the dark evil that misbalanced the universe's ecology"...." Consumerism, and Industrial Revolution brought about a downfall in human values, by creating stories how materialistic wealth could bring happiness & hoarding of wealth initiated bridging and widening the gap between rich and poor."..."Literally, all packaged stuff is unhealthy but has been promoted as healthy, by sweet stories and words"

• xii •

Foreword

In an era of seeking personal growth and global change, readers are empowered to cut through life's clutter and unlock their cosmic potential. As the audience, they're the change-makers the world needs. The cosmic journey awaits, offering inspiration to a world craving transformation.

This diverse book embarks on a profound journey of self-discovery, aiming to unveil innate potential by addressing clutter, be it mental or societal. Originating from the author's deeply personal response to his daughter's letter, it champions independence, personal growth, and curiosity, challenging conventional education systems. The book explores human development, the role of thoughts in shaping reality, the Universal Law of Love, and the connection between individual choices and global issues like consumerism and climate change. It delves into higher consciousness, impending technocratic challenges, and the need to reduce one's carbon footprint, inspiring readers to awaken their creativity and make positive contributions to the world.

Preface

In the twilight of my years, I find myself pondering the mysteries of life, both my own and the grand tapestry of existence itself. It is a journey that began with a letter, a heartfelt missive from my daughter that set in motion the wheels of reflection and revelation.

"Who can know me better than I do?" This question, a common refrain, has echoed in the hearts of countless souls. Yet, I have come to realise that the answer is not as simple as it may seem. To truly comprehend oneself, we must first embark on a quest for the fundamental truths of our existence. Who are we? From whence have we come? What lies within the depths of our souls, guiding our every step?

The inquiry then extends to the very essence of life itself. What, indeed, is an organism? Life on this Earth, be it in the form of plants, animals, or humankind, is united by this label – "organism." It signifies a living entity, possessing an intricate structure, capable of reacting to stimuli, reproducing, growing, adapting, and maintaining equilibrium. All living beings, whether composed of a single cell or a multitude, fall under this classification. From towering trees to humble fungi, from the microscopic to the majestic, the spectrum of life is a wondrous tapestry. Yet, amidst this diversity, a perplexing enigma persists. We contemplate the cosmos, a celestial mind of perfection, and we contemplate the human brain, a marvel of excellence. One orchestrates the harmony of the universe, while the other orchestrates the harmonious workings of our mortal vessels. Both possess the remarkable ability to repair and rejuvenate. Then why, we must ask, does our world seem so entrenched in chaos? Why do humans, endowed with such intelligence, struggle to unite humanity and the Earth, of which they are an integral part?

To unravel this enigma, we must journey back through the annals of time, to an era when humanity believed itself to be the pinnacle of creation, capable of shaping its destiny both in this life and the hereafter. Yet, I must share a revelation that may astonish many: humans, too, belong to this vast family of organisms. Furthermore, every organism, from the tiniest cell to the most complex life form, possesses a body, a mind, and a soul – a triumvirate essential for survival. In their quest for existence, they all partake in the intricate dance of the food chain and web, each one relying on the other for sustenance. This, students of biology understand well.

But what sets humans apart from the multitude of other organisms? It is not on the physical, mental, conscious, or even soulful plane. Both share physical forms, both possess minds and consciousness, and both house souls.

Humans have the capacity for profound thought, motivated by instincts, intellect, and logic. Unlike animals, who follow their instincts without the benefit of reason, we possess the power of contemplation. Consider, for instance, the behaviours deeply ingrained in our nature. They unfold predictably in response to the appropriate stimuli, regardless of prior experience. It is a testament to the intricate web of instincts that guide us. If we concede that all organisms, whether solitary cells or conglomerates of life possess consciousness, then we must also acknowledge the presence of a soul within each. The divergence between humans and the rest of the organic world does not lie in the physical, mental, or spiritual realms. It lies in the realm of self-awareness, a rare gift bestowed upon humanity alone. The conundrum, however, is that despite our awareness and intellect, our knowledge remains incomplete. For decades, humanity has teetered on the precipice of uncertainty, ignorant of our true nature and purpose. We navigate life's turbulent waters without a compass, resulting in chaos and disconnection from our authentic selves.

When one is adrift in the sea of uncertainty, unaware of their origins, composition, and purpose, confusion reigns supreme, and actions lack direction. It is in this fog of ignorance that humanity has stumbled, unable to wield its intelligence wisely.

This book, a mosaic of themes and revelations, delves into the profound facets of existence. It beckons us to explore biology, the very science of life, and to understand our place within this intricate web of organisms. It invites us to manifest our deepest desires and nurture our internal motivation, igniting the sparks of creativity that reside within us. It extols the virtue of being one with nature and the cosmos, for therein lies our true harmony. It warns against the siren call of consumerism and technocracy, urging us to declutter our lives and preserve the precious gift of nature.

In these pages, you will find the keys to unlock the door to a purposeful life, a life lived in harmony with the natural world and the cosmos. For in understanding ourselves, we unlock the potential to harness our intelligence for the greater good of all.

Prologue

In an era of seeking personal growth and global change, readers are empowered to cut through life's clutter and unlock their cosmic potential. As the audience, they're the change-makers the world needs. The cosmic journey awaits, offering inspiration to a world craving transformation.

This diverse book embarks on a profound journey of self-discovery, aiming to unveil innate potential by addressing clutter, be it mental or societal. Originating from the author's deeply personal response to his daughter's letter, it champions independence, personal growth, and curiosity, challenging conventional education systems. The book explores human development, the role of thoughts in shaping reality, the Universal Law of Love, and the connection between individual choices and global issues like consumerism and climate change. It delves into higher consciousness, impending technocratic challenges, and the need to reduce one's carbon footprint, inspiring readers to awaken their creativity and make positive contributions to the world.

CHAPTER ONE

WAY TO WISDOM

Guilt is a powerful emotion. It arises when the better part of the self strongly condemns the wrong actions committed earlier. However, sometimes, you make mistakes but do not realize them. Mia Culpa, I am guilty. I became aware of my blunder after going through your letter. It was very unsettling. It shook the core of my being. A surge of guilt ran through my body. You were offended by me not sharing the experiences of Life with you - those who love the most hurt the most. That guilt generated a pang of love and a strong urge to tell you everything truthfully. I tried but failed miserably - penning my experiences in a few pages was impossible.

Deepak Chopra says you can't learn wisdom like you learn maths. Wisdom is like growing up. It's not like your genes making you a kid, but something you choose to do. Wisdom is a journey that can't be taught or learned. I started my journey of Wisdom early in phases. I intend to take you through those phases, but Wisdom can't be achieved just by experiencing or reading the experiences of others. You must peek inside and watch within with full consciousness to know your true self and make the right choices. I intend to make you wise, which ultimately takes you to a state of knowingness. Your wisdom encompasses all: your understanding is limitless. Understand yourself to break free from everything that restrains, troubles, confuses, and brings despair.

....

Earlier, I often tried to share my experiences but always felt helpless. I felt helpless as I didn't know how to communicate with you about the realities of Life. One reason is my strained relationship with your mum; naturally, your closeness to her and her beliefs distanced me from you.   My continuous failure in business was another deterrent. My mad adherence to philosophical thoughts was poles apart from the belief system of my relatives, including your mum, of which you became a part. You spent time among your people who were loving and caring. Your days were full of joy, and you enjoyed every moment of Life free from worries. I, too, was happy to see you, though I wanted a little time to exchange philosophical ideas but had not the courage to disturb the festive moments you were enjoying. I was sure that the people you spend most of your time with were critical of my aloofness and stubbornness for not agreeing with the so-called 'sageness' of elders they shared with you. When all of them sang the same tune, it was inconceivable for you to consider them wrong. You sang along. You had no idea that reality could be different.

When millions of people repeat a statement for thousands of years, views are accepted as accurate. And when expressions based on death and foreboding fill people's minds with fear, people cannot be bold enough to ask questions to know reality. You, too, became a victim of this group and never took the courage to investigate and find the truth. It was too late when I realised that you had already been under the grip of that fear. I found myself in a bind. I knew it would be impossible to bring you into a thoughtful confabulation. But my subconscious mind looked for an opportunity. Too much time had passed under the river since, and I almost lost all hope. But, finally, I got inspiration from your letter, which gave me the idea of expressing my experiences by writing a book.

You know about my different notion of Life from everyone here. My being different was not accepted by my people - I was too curious. My awareness level was a bit high. I knew what people thought about me. I was not a business success. People perceived that a person like me, who failed for decades, couldn't achieve success, ever - "once a failure is always a failure" couldn't be further from the truth". I was very much conscious of the thoughts taking place in their minds. They were baffled and awed by my carefree lifestyle. They feared the Path I was treading and wanted me to return to the fold. Naturally, I was forced to keep a distance from everyone who mattered much to me. Another cause of the deterrent was my lack of articulation of my ideas. My impaired eye vision was another reason. These things made me remain low-key.

Am I really a hardened failure? "Jim's Gems" by Jim Smith has a different story.   Lots fear failure, but it won't block success. Failing can even lead to success if we learn. It's a key to success and teaches us plenty. Thomas Edison may be the greatest inventor of the modern era, said the following while on his journey to create the long-lasting electric light bulb, "I've not failed. I have just found 10,000 ways that won't work." My failures made me gain some wisdom. You may have heard that 'wisdom is gained through experience'. So was with me.

No doubt, it is beyond the capacity of the outer world to assess a person's experiences, and the deciding factor of one's success or failure is the quality of experiences one has. You are unsuccessful if you can't make enough money to live a comfortable life. Thomas Edison failed 10,000 times. In the eyes of the outer world, he was a failure, but he was "committed to success" Jim's Gems continues,
Well, you see, there could be many reasons for it. Some might be clear as day, like marrying the boss's daughter, but it could also be something less obvious, like being super dedicated to success.

I have always been committed to success, and I failed. Maybe, I failed because of my low vision, feeble-mindedness, absent mind and lack of business acumen, but my failures taught me valuable lessons. I am still committed to success because failures allow me to learn. I am so used to failures that it doesn't cause any distress to me. Instead, it keeps my mind healthy and active. Most, who have gained success materialistically, are disconnected from ground realities. They fear the unpredictableness of Life and ignore the greater purpose of Life. For real success, you have to be critical of yourself. I have always been a self-critic.

Book writing is challenging for me, who has been very poor at studies. But inspiration can do wonders, and no one can inspire me more than you. My love for you has always been infinite and unconditional. Putting conditions for love is unrealistic. "Real love is when you feel ecstatic in every moment." Conditional love means putting demands on others. The way my people wished for me to merge with their culture. Have I ever put any requests on you? I don't remember. I only wanted to see you stand tall and be true to yourself.

Bestowing unconditional love is the fundamental nature of every living thing. It is the nature of the organism; we, too, are an organism – a multicellular organism. The building blocks of our body are cell organisms. There are 30-40 trillion cells in your body. You can find this unconditional giving nature in nature. "Nature gives lavishly and never expects anything in return. It gives Life, gives joy, gives Wisdom, and it asks for no payback. Even when humans decimate their resources, nature keeps finding new ways of giving. Even if we practiced a fraction of the generosity of nature, imagine how different the world would be. Look what would happen with love like that; it would light up the world with kindness. Sufi mystic Hafiz said, "Even after all this time, the sun never says to the earth, "You owe me." Love like that lights up the whole sky.``- source article "Learn From Nature" by Pushpa Chaturvedi. You know, every human is born with many innate capacities. One of them is to lend a helping hand to others. You can find this instinct present even in children. Watch how they try to help their parents and friends. This inborn sense remains all through Life. Don't you feel so when you see deprived people needing help anywhere in the world? You think so because of the universal love found in every human being since birth. This love is inborn, not learned. What knowledge is gained extrinsically can be true or untrue; you have to prove it; Intrinsic knowledge is proper knowledge; we get proper motivation.   But the victims of cultures think otherwise.

No doubt your letter caused the spark to write this book. Nevertheless, my love for humanity gave me another spark. Won't it be a matter of great contentment when ill-advised people are awakened to the complex realities of Life after reading my book?

....

What is the significance of 'good part of the self' and 'truthfulness' in Life? The best self is the inner self, core self, true nature, essential nature, soul, heart consciousness etc. Our essential genetic nature; is an inborn gift endowed to all human beings and a natural source of truthfulness. The truth is inside all of us; we are aware of it. From my very childhood, subconsciously, I have been close to my true self, intuitively but unaware, but now I am very much aware. Unaware, all humans refer to their natural selves. Not a day passes without problems; problems could be trivial or complex. You intuitively and primarily unconsciously refer to your core self to resolve the issues. Faced with such issues, you often seek space to search your soul – soul searching - by going into deep thoughts to incubate and choose an apt solution among several solutions. The outer world often offers solutions, but the best and final decision lies with you – consciously or subconsciously – you refer to your true self before making a final decision. Babies can't be taught anything at birth, and their every action is intuitive, and the source of intuition is nothing but their inborn natural reality.

Of course, they make mistakes, but they learn fast only from them. To stop them from making mistakes means stopping them from learning; they need wise mentoring, not teaching.

CHAPTER TWO

COSMIC MIND

"Panpsychism is the view that everything has a mind or a mind-like quality. The word itself was coined by the Italian philosopher Francesco Patrizi in the sixteenth century and derived from the two Greek words pan (all) and psyche (soul or mind). This definition is quite general and raises two immediate questions: (1) What does one mean by "all things"? (2) What does one mean by "mind"? Some philosophers propose that everything in the universe, big or small, might have a touch of consciousness, a concept known as panpsychism. The origin of consciousness is a big scientific puzzle. In his book "Galileo's Error: Foundations for a New Science of Consciousness," philosopher Philip Goff suggests a radical idea. He thinks that consciousness might not be unique to brains but could be a fundamental quality of all matter, even things like rocks. You can learn more about this in the article "Does Consciousness Pervade the Universe?" It's a pretty thought-provoking concept.

I've been pondering this idea that the whole universe might have this mind-like quality. It's like saying the cosmos itself is intelligent. It's a bit puzzling, but it sure does make you wonder about the world. And there's even more evidence out there to think about. So, I'll keep pondering on this one. That is to say, the cosmos or universe is conscious and intelligent. Cosmos is omnipresent and omniscient. Humans, too, are a part of the cosmos. Hence their birth is cosmic, and their minds are nothing but cosmic. That is, their mind is a cosmic mind. Therefore human consciousness is no different from cosmic consciousness. All knowledge of the universe is inherent in our cosmic mind.

The extraordinary thing about humans is that humans are self-aware. All other things may have a mind-like quality, but except humans, no other thing or being in the whole universe is self-aware; this awareness is the problem. Animals are not self-aware but are guided by their survival instinct; they naturally know and choose all things good for their survival. In contrast, humans do not choose anything without reasoning based on their knowledge and experience, thanks to their intelligence. To be intelligent is good but what is troubling is humans are not fully aware. They are not aware that they are born with a cosmic mind with cosmic intelligence; they don't know that their connection with cosmic intelligence has been disrupted sometimes after their birth. Though they often miss its absence, particularly in their solitary moments, and yearn to reconnect with it. There is a feeling of restlessness because they don't know how to connect. This restiveness is very strong in children who try hard to reconnect. Not able to connect, in desperation, they seek help from everyone around them.

You can notice this wild passion in every child. You can observe their deep, obsessive curiosity: they ask questions endlessly. Children's unspoken, unexplained desire is to reconnect again with cosmic intelligence and find the truth of its relation with life on earth. But children rarely get the correct answer. Instead, they are told stories to mollify their curiosity, whose authenticity is inexact and debatable. When they mistrust, they advocate that not believing the stories is a sin and that sinners are not saved from punishments that scare them stiff. Frightened, children lack the courage to probe the authenticity of stories. This fear remains for the rest of their life. Thus, their minds get conditioned with the stories in time, and the truth never comes to light. As a result, most people remain ignorant all their lives.

The unbelievable advancement of conventional science in panpsychism makes it possible to unravel many mysteries of existence. That is the purpose of this book; to investigate, solve and explain cosmic reality and its relation with the world and humans. For many, words like cosmic consciousness, cosmic intelligence, or universal intelligence would be strange. But people who are well acquainted with the ways of spirituality/philosophy would find these terms familiar because spiritualists have never been disconnected or have been able to reconnect with cosmic or universal intelligence. The good news is that anyone with solid ambitions and intense curiosity and desire can reconnect with it. And can bring back harmony, unity, integrity and peace missing from their lives. We missed it because we have been caught in the thick of thin things, which made our lives anxious. We felt out of control. Fortunately, though, not consciously but habitually, I never disconnected from cosmic consciousness because I never believed these adopted stories told and repeatedly retold to us for thousands of years. How I was not affected by these stories and what enabled me to keep the connection with cosmic consciousness is my story that began, perhaps, in my teens.

Life could be simple for most people, but for me, it has been like a jigsaw puzzle with millions of pieces. All my life, I have been trying to put the pieces together. The complete picture of a jigsaw puzzle emerges when you can put all the pieces together. We piece together a jigsaw puzzle consulting the picture on the cover, but the reference point of life's puzzle is your true self, your genuine natural self. It took almost all my life to solve the puzzle. Now, I know a lot of it, and it would be unwise of me if I didn't tell you the whole story, truthfully. I have to flashback to what happened. That gave me a different perspective. That is crucial because you are not aware of many things about me. And unless you know my personality inside out, you won't be able to appreciate my story.

Humans are born intelligent with a cosmic knowledge/innate knowledge to perceive different colours, sounds, smells, tastes and feelings without training or experience. He can also distinguish between truth and untruth, wrong or right, and beauty and ugliness. His understanding of truth is innate, not learned. The Innate Knowledge idea says we have knowledge right from the start like it's built into us. We don't need experiences to know it, and it's not from learning or thinking. It's just there.

Now, when it comes to our connection with the big cosmic intelligence, we humans are in the dark. But, naturally, we're a curious bunch. We want to know it all, and that's why kids are so nosy and curious – it's in their nature. They ask millions of questions about life, about everything. Unfortunately, the majority of them don't get the truth. They are told stories; that the people believe in. But a few do not believe and investigate to find the truth. They are usually called spiritualists. I, too, never believed those stories. Possibly it was the unconditional love of my parents that gave me the freedom to be prying.

Your grandfather was an honest man. He drew admiration for his integrity and empathy. He was an attentive listener, and his generosity is still remembered. I never saw him being enraged. Of course, sometimes he got irritated but came to himself quickly. Though not literate, he had the characteristics of a "king's energy". He has been very generous toward the poor. My parents, especially my mother, loved me unconditionally. Being my mother's first child from my father's second marriage, my mother's love for me was unconditionally genuine. She never put any condition for her love except that I shouldn't be disrespectful to elders. Being free from constraints allowed me to think and do anything I desired. Though I didn't disrespect anyone, I was a curious boy requiring proof of stories people around told me. When I disbelieved the truth of the stories, I felt that people didn't like my scepticism, which obliged me to keep myself low-key. I never believed in the stories as they seemed unrealistic to me. That was a problematic situation because everyone believed those stories except me. Still, I did not have a strained relationship with anyone. I always have high regard for my people and receive the same from everyone. But there were unspoken, unexpressed strange, uneasy feelings that lingered that made me and others restive. Elders, who thought they knew everything, didn't like my inquisitiveness. They felt uncomfortable with my interrogations because they didn't know the answer and feared going beyond what they perceived as the ultimate truth. I was duty-bound to keep silent as I saw their countenance of being vexed at my persistence. They expected me to accept whatever they believed. Any discussion was iffy. After some time, I stopped asking. But the questions stayed in my subconscious mind, and I looked for the answer elsewhere. Sometimes, it took years to arrive at the solution, but I always found the truth. I never accepted anything without getting to the bottom of the truth.

I have been an incoherent child – an absent-minded, slow learner, primarily self-absorbed. I was unenthusiastic and a dullard for all my life. In my childhood, I was always reluctant to participate in games and was poor in my studies. I remained a poor student even in senior classes. In my teens, though, I survived smallpox, a lethal virus, but not without a heavy toll. I had opaque eyes with nearly no vision on my right and reduced vision on my left. It was hard for me to recognize the sharpness of a person's facial features beyond 10 feet. I never felt comfortable with people around me, and neither did I have friends of value because their talks were always confusing and unclear subjects, and there was a sameness. Or my involvement was more like a silent spectator, and I was attentive only when the issues were logical, which was rare.

The only thing that interested me most was reading detective novels. I liked their intrigue, which kept me guessing their logical end, the outcome of which was often shocking. I also was fond of reading business magazines and management books which gave me insight into a complex situation or problem and gained a deep understanding of problems. I also liked watching movies in the cinemas. The 60s and 70s were said to be the golden era of Indian movies; they mostly were classics and intelligent, representing life's lessons. I couldn't participate in sports because of my visual impediment; I had few schools or college friends. Studies never interest me. Anyhow, I graduated after failing several times.

My parents were not literate, yet my father was a successful businessman. He was a simple carpet weaver, a cottage industry product from his teens. He wove for an Englishman who understood the dialect well enough to interact with locals. Impressed by my father's honesty, simplicity and insight, the Englishman made him a contractor for supplying carpets; thus, he became a small-time businessman. As the business grew, he established a firm in partnership with his three brothers. After that, the company grew with the help of an accountant and a few helpers he employed. Later his two sons from his first marriage joined. After that, business took a natural growth. He was among the top exporters of carpets in town during the late 50s and 60s.

Fortunately, when I was graduating, my roommate happened to be a brilliant post-graduation - English literature student - which attracted other brilliant scholars whose discussions were primarily philosophical, riveting my attention. These discussions left a deep impression on my psyche. After that, I started reading philosophical articles, fiction and nonfiction. I also read a few books on management. After graduation, I read some books by spiritualist Dr Deepak Chopra, making me an even more rational thinker. Years later, I purchased a smartphone; it was a boon for me because my reading speed was languid. I started watching videos by Deepak Chopra and other spiritualists and philosophical speakers, which acquainted me with quantum physics, quantum entanglement and panpsychism. While writing this book, I had to do deep research, which has genuinely opened my inner eye.

After going through these involvements, I became keener to learn about life's puzzles and mysteries of existence. I wanted to discover what soul spirit is. Humans know that they cannot exist without a soul and spirit, but it is such an utterly perplexing subject that most people are disquieted at mentioning the words soul or spirit. But I had a fascination with these terms. I dwelled deeply to understand what spirituality is and the purpose of spiritualism. I concluded that every human is born with a soul spirit. I also learned that the cosmos is not devoid of soul and spirit, known as cosmic consciousness, universal consciousness, or universal intelligence, and It is a scientific worldview. Cosmos has no boundaries; it is present everywhere. It is also present in humans as well. We often connect with cosmic intelligence and experience soul consciousness when we are heart-conscious because the heart is the centre of the soul, and soul consciousness is no different from cosmic consciousness.

Spiritualists are heart-conscious or soul-conscious and connected with cosmic intelligence. They are connected because they know how to connect. Connecting with heart consciousness means connecting with cosmic intelligence, universal intelligence, or the spirit soul. Ordinary people connect now and then, but neither know nor are aware of it. It is just a matter of awareness; every human keeps connecting with heart consciousness but only when he is in trouble or faced with challenging life problems. In trouble, he wants a little space to live with himself - in silence to connect with his heart and examine the problem deeply. In solitude, he disconnects from worldly affairs and becomes free from all constraints; in that freedom, you are in your heart's consciousness.

The entrepreneurial bug bit me in my final year of graduation (1968). I had made up my mind to enter the carpet business separately. By then, the family had become too large to accommodate everyone. Trade, too, was not as rampant as it used to be. My elderly father was not active enough, and my two half-brothers were at the company helm. They obliged my request to establish a new firm. The carpet industry is a cottage industry that requires understanding to deal with illiterate weavers. My inexperience, visual problems, and soft nature were enough to write off my success. But I continued. My madness distanced me from my wife as I sold her ornaments. I also sold inherited properties to invest in, but success has always been illusory.

On June 1, 2014, I had discomfort in my chest and exhaustion afterwards. I was confident of a heart stroke. It was worrying. I was health-conscious and always tried to take care of my health. Possibly, stress was the cause of discomfort. I was pretty confident that I had to go for stent surgery. Fortunately, the doctor was not in a hurry and prescribed drugs to my relief. I was under his treatment for a few months without any relief. In the meantime, I was busy googling for the best alternative remedial practice for ailing hearts and found Ayurveda, whose treatment relieved me. I took more care of my health. But I often felt uneasiness in my chest. I tried Naturopathy and learned a few more valuable things about self-care. But more than that, googling gave several helpful tips for self-care.

....

During your school and college years, you cherished the freedom to think and act as your heart desired, remaining intimately connected to the wisdom within your heart and cosmic intelligence. After completing your education, both of you embarked on the journey of marriage. Before that, we engaged in open-hearted conversations, a rarity in our culture. It's not common to find such amiability between fathers and daughters in a conservative society where fear sets the boundaries of modesty and decency. Many young adults set out to explore the world, guided by their inner callings or the wisdom of capable mentors, which helps them recognize their unique potential and attain great heights.

Throughout your school and college days, your intuition served as your trusted guide, and your curiosity was boundless. You carried an attitude that proclaimed, "I know nothing; how can I know everything?" However, marriage brought about a significant transformation. You had to adapt to new circumstances, forming deep emotional bonds with your life partners. Love was experienced on emotional, mental, and spiritual levels, and you freely shared your thoughts and feelings. You embraced the familiar and comforting aspects of your new culture, settling into a routine that minimized stress and provided a sense of mental security. This resulted in a state of regular happiness, reduced anxiety, and less stress, something that typically brings contentment to parents, especially for their daughters. Nevertheless, there were moments when I felt restless, yearning to share life's hidden truths with you, truths that might have remained concealed. However, unveiling these realities meant pushing you beyond your comfort zone, a daunting task that I knew would make you uneasy and uncomfortable.

In the past, you were open-minded individuals who relished engaging in debates whenever differing opinions arose. Diverse perspectives allowed for fruitful discussions and enhanced your wisdom and resilience. However, now there seems to be a reluctance to engage in deliberation, as some have come to believe that troubles are meant for others and not for themselves. This attitude of unpreparedness often catches people off guard when life's challenges strike and it is this unpreparedness that can be the root cause of many of life's difficulties.

After 25/30, people develop a mindset of their own, and if a belief system influences you, you start to fear the uncertain future. You fear participating in any talk that is not in line with the belief system. I am afraid you were tricked into becoming a part of this system. You were no more curious than you used to be during your academia, free from social mores. Then you were always ready to face challenges. Now you feared the unknown unrealistic future - the fear which made you reserved. That made my task nearly impossible.

....

During my life, one thing was constantly with me. I never lost touch with my core self, my cosmic mind. My closeness to my true self kept me far from the family culture, though it was painful for everyone. But for me, it was highly satisfying. I knew what my people expected: they wanted me to follow their culture. A culture that was based on beliefs and had no scientific base. I slowly disengaged from these assemblies, except for yearly fests or marriage ceremonies, which was hard for me. When I was a total failure in business, I felt like living like an alien. They thought I was selfish. But nothing made me change because something made me uncomfortable about their beliefs. They were surprised by my behaviour. They thought I was treading on a path that was full of hazards. I felt like an outcast. Of course, no one disrespected me, but they looked baffled as if I was a strange species that had forgotten its way and landed among them. At the same time, consternation prevented them from having face-to-face confabulation with me

CHAPTER THREE

GIFT OF FREEDOM

The "Spring Board of Success" article on the Shattuck-St Mary's School website in Malaysia starts by mentioning research from The Association of Boarding Schools. It says that boarding school grads are more likely to reach top management roles in their later careers compared to private and public school graduates I'm grateful that you both had the chance to go to boarding schools and spend your entire educational journey away from home, starting from primary school and going all the way through graduation. It sounds like those were the best times of your lives. Time was great simply because of the freedom you enjoyed. Independence to be free to act, speak or think as you will, free from any pressure or obligations. You never felt lacking anything and always lived in the moment. There was no compulsion except rules set by the boarding house to give you a sense of responsibility and discipline. Otherwise, you receive good guidance, including studies, sports and extracurricular activities opportunities, and fewer distractions, making you focus on problems and take action independently.

Humans are born free, but they are almost always made captive by some cultural mores. If a child is free and lives under some adroit guidance, it can perform wonders. However social restraints suppress freedom by applying strict social norms. Let's take a look at what the website "Tranquil Freedom" says about freedom:

In our culture, my dear, true freedom comes when we embrace the universe and all living beings as a part of our own existence. When we exclude others, we limit our freedom and diminish our shared humanity. To be truly free, we must include everyone. Throughout your educational journey and career, you embraced this philosophy, and that's why you experienced genuine freedom. As the wise Roger Gabriel puts it, "Everything in the universe is connected." However, our daily routines can sometimes make us forget this profound truth.

Roger, he's a wise soul, you see. He speaks of living as if you are the entire universe, finding joy in the present moment, transcending past and future. It's about boundless peace, eternal harmony, and unconditional love. Picture a world without fear, where equality prevails in all things – that's the essence of Oneness. You, my dear, lived in the present and found oneness and true freedom. Your path is one to be admired and respected in our culture.

You naturally lived in the now and practised oneness throughout your schooling – from primary till graduation – free from the mundane humdrum. You practised living harmoniously with all and experienced oneness.   There was no sense of duality. You are in love with everything, including yourself, when you include everything. You nourish your soul when you are in love with everything. That takes your being on a higher plane, and you savour life meaningfully. Another way to understand oneness or inclusiveness is to know that everything in the world is made of five elements - earth, water, fire, wind and void. All elements are made up of atoms, the building blocks of all kinds of stuff. Atoms are energy particles. You see, science teaches us that everything is crafted from energy. It's the very foundation of all matter. The same energy that forms your body is also the very essence of the bricks in your home, your car, your phone, and even the living creatures and trees around us. It's all one and the same – energy.

So, where does the difference come in? Well, the difference lies in the ego mind of us humans. Without that ego, there's oneness. Without it, there's no distinction or difference to be found.

Life cannot thrive without the support of these five elements. Every human or non-human life is made of these five elements. Whether conscious or not, every second, your body is nourished by these elements by eating, drinking, breathing, and getting energy from the sun and space - all of these keep you in high spirits. Then why exclude anyone?

You instinctively yearned to live harmoniously with everyone in your boarding life - students, teachers, staff workers, or anyone; you name it. You instinctively and naively longed for inclusiveness. You may have noticed uneasiness whenever there was a lack of coherence with your friends or anybody. When your heart, your true self, lacks tranquillity, you feel restless. Tranquillity is impossible without inclusiveness. When there is any disturbance, you seek ways to return to tranquil moments - this is the law of nature, and you are part of nature. Whenever there's a disturbance in nature, all its elements come together to restore harmony. Remember, "After every storm, there is a rainbow." You, my dear, savour nature most in its pristine form. Your mind remains restless and disturbed as long as you are at loggerheads. Our minds act best when free and in a state of restfulness. Inclusiveness, that's the mantra to success. Exclusion, well, that's what causes conflicts all around the world.

You know, there's a saying by Pablo Picasso: "Action is the Foundational Key to All Success." It means you've got to take action to make things happen. Just dreaming and hoping won't cut it. You need to do something. And it's true, my dear, action is the key to success. Our thoughts lead to our actions. As the Late President of the Bi-Lo Stores, Frank Outlaw once said,

"Watch your thoughts, they become words; watch your words, they become actions; watch your actions, they become habits; watch your habits, they become character; watch your character, for it becomes your destiny."

What is important is to watch - watch your thoughts, words, actions, habits, and characters. This watching is best when you have the freedom and are in a state of inclusiveness. If your thoughts are under any obligation, measures cannot be high-yielding. Happily, you were as free as the air in your longboarding life. You were free from beholden. Children are highly motivated from within. However, their motivation works best when they are free to give feedback and make decisions independently. Theresa V Wilson, in her article called "Being Inspired From Within," says something interesting: "By tapping into the inspiration within, you can uncover the true essence of your calling. Keep in mind, it's a step-by-step process, and each step should be completed." It's all about finding your path by looking deep inside.

Just imagine, for over one and a half decades, you had the freedom and enjoyed the inclusive environment; you were favoured to use your free will to choose whatever you desired. And the great thing about it was that you never choose anything unprincipled or fraudulent. You had the freedom, yet you always made the right decision. How come you were never unfair? Who was your guide? The simple answer is that you tapped your true self; your true self or heart was the guide, And "the heart is also conceived of as the locus of moral sense." You never made any decision without referring to it, though, not consciously. You referred to it subconsciously before making any decisions or taking action, and the signals you received gave you great lessons.

Throughout your life, there's been a little inner guide giving you advice, sometimes softly, sometimes insistently. You can call it what you want: inner voice, inner wisdom, or something else. This guide isn't always a voice you hear; it's often a feeling or hunch, maybe an image or impression. That's why folks say, "Listen to your gut." Your body knows the truth; it's like a trustworthy compass, as Rachelle Williams wisely tells us.

If you take a peek at the past, you may recall that my advice to you often used to be, "be yourself" while leaving home for boarding, especially when you arrived at adolescence. Then, I knew the power of true self - your inner voice and its being linked to freedom. I knew that you would never falter as long as you were near your inner voice. Unaware, you were. But now, I realise that unless you are imbued with the deeper meaning of "be yourself", the advice is not understood in its true sense. You heard me say it, but you didn't know its significance. Neither was I smart enough to foresee the perils of half-knowledge.

You needed a meaningful and well-founded explanation to bring home the limitless power of the true self. I lament for not being proficient enough to teach you what "be yourself" really means. As I mentioned earlier, since childhood I have been a slow learner and lacked the skill of oral communication. Back then, my own learning, too, was not mature. I strongly believe that had I been fully aware of these nuances, I might have imparted some meaning of being yourself, and you would have been much more bright and far-sighted, inspiring thousands, if not millions, of people. I say so with absolute certainty simply because I know thousands of wise men, women, boys and girls who outshine and far exceed the understanding of millions. Thanks to the intelligent parenting or mentoring they received from their enlightened parents/mentors, they are now highly intuitive, and their awareness of self is remarkable. Child, remember this: "Standing up for what you believe in" matters most. You see when you don't stand for something, you can fall for anything. Standing up for your beliefs means having faith in your true self, and what can be more exhilarating than that? It's great to explore the world and learn from others, but the real magic happens when you take what's out there and mix it with your own creative thinking. As Sheila McCann rightly says, that's when things get powerful and dynamic.

"Mistakes are proof that you are trying", and you make hundreds of mistakes every day. Thanks to your independence, you frequently resorted to your free will and benefited greatly from it. First, you learn to cope well with your mistakes. Second, you become free from fear; third, your personality evolves fast. Above all, you enjoyed your days of error and correction. There was a feeling that you were complete and never lacked anything, always confident that you could turn your desires into reality simply because you had the ability to take responsibility.

You failed hundreds of times in other areas of your activity. Still, failures have become a routine, and you accept them without any fuss because every failure generates new ideas, and you enjoy it. Your disappointments made you a bit wiser. You were always ready to face the challenge. Your mind was focused and attentive. Recall how the alert was in your mind when on the playground; you made mistakes. In a split second, your true self notices your mistake, generates ideas for the next move, registers the cause of the error on your memory and saves you from repeating it. You see, sometimes we tend to focus more on our failures than our successes. As Andy Stanley puts it in his article, "Your Life is a Treasure Chest," your failures can actually make you wiser, especially when teaching the next generation. You learn a lot from failing, more than from succeeding. Remember,   inaction doesn't get you results. When you take action, whether you fail or succeed, you gain experience. As Theodore Roosevelt said, "The only man who never makes mistakes is the man who never does anything." So, keep your mind active with actions and reflections, don't let it get lazy with inaction. In boarding, you were always active, whether mentally or physically.

Besides mistakes, you must have encountered moments of anxiety in your long life in boarding schools. At such times, your mind sought a little solitude for self-talk - a dialogue with your inner voice. Hundreds of ideas enter your mind with clarity when your mind is quiet and at peace; the way the details of the skies reflect on the placid waters of a lake, ideas enter into a restful mind. After a while, you come out illuminated with new ideas. You have discovered the new person in you with a little more confidence and a bright smile spread all over your face. No one can give you honest guidance except your true self in hard times. That moment of silence mostly gave you the best solution to your problems. Perhaps you are not familiar with the expression, "You create your reality." But you have always created your reality during schooling guided by your inner voice, which made life thrilling. That was possible simply because you had the freedom to be close to the source of your power - your core natural self – and the freedom to use your free will.

For thoughtful and purposeful strategic planning, you need a calm, tranquil mind to reflect and let the ideas flood in. Humans have great potential, but it doesn't come easy. You have to work hard to achieve your full potential. The cause is a lack of awareness about the potency of your true self. Though naturally, I have been very close to my core self since childhood, I became aware of its reality quite late in life. Children under the guidance of conscious parents, who have thorough knowledge about the fundamental nature of the human core, never miss the race of turning their dreams into reality. There are very few schools in the world where children are made aware of the secret of their unique core values, which enable them to exploit their potential to the fullest. Anyways, it is "better to be late than never". You are still capable of manipulating your potential. You have to make some serious moves.

There are many examples where even the poorest of the poor attained unimaginable heights, Simply because they were not under any pressure or bound by any obligations. To be a top-class sportsperson or a professional, you need years of failures that hone your skill. The experience you gain from your losses gives you a beautiful feeling and happiness with the knowledge of your experience. That is the way of evolution—that is how humans evolve. But evolution is quite fast; when you are conscious of your own consciousness, you are aware of your thoughts, emotions, motives, experiences, etc. In full awareness, you do not miss the effect of every event occurring. In movies, a character is often seen communicating with his self-image projected at a distance to evaluate his own value. To understand yourself better, you need to practise self-awareness. It means watching and feeling your thoughts and emotions from a distance. Dr. Tasha Eurich, a respected psychologist and author, explains that self-awareness lets you see yourself clearly, understand how others perceive you, and fit into the world. It's like having a superpower. People who are self-aware, tend to have fulfilling lives, strong relationships, creativity, confidence, and effective communication. They're also more ethical, perform better at work, and lead more successful companies. So, my dear, practising self-awareness is a valuable journey.

Parents at large are pretty worried about the future of their offspring. But wise parents, who know the strength of their inner self, know how to bring out the best in their children and create an environment around them that can help them understand themselves. They know the learning of babies starts even before their birth. In the last trimester of gestation, unborn babies begin learning language and music. You'll be amazed by what babies can learn before they're born. There's a study from 1988 that even suggests newborns can recognize their mom's favourite soap opera theme song. More recent studies show that they get familiar with their parents' language too. For instance, American newborns find Swedish vowels strange, and Swedish babies feel the same about English vowels, as Beth Skwarecki mentions in her article "Babies

Learning in the Womb." Incredible, isn't it?

Unaware, you frequently notice witnessing your own thoughts, activities and emotions. You see, it's crucial to observe your own thoughts and feelings. By changing how you interpret things in your mind, you can change your emotions. This self-awareness is a key part of Emotional Intelligence, and it can lead to success.

It's like the "I" in you, your superconscious mind, keeping an eye on your thoughts. As the Oxford Dictionary says, self-awareness is understanding your character, feelings, motives, and desires. It's recognizing yourself as a separate individual from the world around you. That's the essence of it.

You were not conscious of your own consciousness, but the "gift of freedom" enabled you to access the power of your inner voice, and you lived a life full of vitality and excitement. Near your genuine self, your personality evolves at a good pace. You lacked nothing. You didn't seek approval from others because you had complete faith in your intentions. Every moment of yours was exciting, lively and stimulating. From the moment your ear heard the matron's call early in the morning to the stern voice reminding the time to bed, your brain was at its creative best without any fear. What is regrettable is that you were not aware of the immense power of your essential nature. Even more unfortunate is that I was not familiar enough to pass this knowledge on to you.

Then your marriage happened. Both of you got the best matches, and you were happy. Your mom and I were glad to find the ideal and well-established man in your life. Your hubbies were successful businessmen. They were loving and caring. I couldn't guess they were unaware of the divine aspects of existence for a long time. Neither were they interested in knowing the metaphysical. That troubled me because life is meaningless without knowing the laws of nature and the purpose of life. They all seem to think it is beyond the human mind to know the grand scheme of gods - a self-deceptive condition programmed in them since childhood. I was at a loss in their loss and their conviction of the outdated models. I tried to bring the topic to the fore. Knowing their minds well about me, I was unnoticed. I also lacked the oral skills to articulate things effectively and felt helpless. They feared knowing the unknown. Then your letter happened, which was no less than a godsend. It inspired me to write this book.

Peter Eyerer and Cristian-Mihai Pomohasi both believe that learning is inherent in human nature. It starts even before birth and continues throughout our lives. Teaching others is also a natural part of being human. I've always had a strong desire to share the lessons I've learned with you. Learning, my dear, never stops. It sparks ideas, and ideas come from self-control. Deepak Chopra, a wise soul, says the secret to self-control is living in the present moment. Among all living creatures, only we humans are aware of the world around us and what's happening inside – our thoughts and emotions. That inner awareness is self-awareness.

You see, the only things we can truly control in life are our thoughts, feelings, and actions. If we master those, we can reach our goals and find success. To gain this kind of control, we must understand the patterns behind our emotions and thoughts, and learn how to manage them, as the article on "How to Manage Your Thoughts, Feelings, and Behaviors" wisely points out.

Only human beings are endowed with the gift of self-awareness. You are not entirely self-aware if you're not looking at the cause of your happiness or anger. But when you are self-aware, you will ask yourself, why do I get angry? Was it a right action or wrong? How does the anger affect my psyche, and can I rein in my anger and act differently when the same situation arises again? Hundreds of such questions occur in your mind when you can watch every activity within your mind that helps you change and improve your personality. "No enemy is more insidious than the one you are blind to." Your worst enemy is your ego inside you. To control it, you need to see what is occurring within you - your thoughts and emotions. When you see things clearly, you can change them.

This self-awareness is crucial for personal evolution. You will get feedback on every action of yours. This way, you will become a critical thinker and understand yourself better daily. This way, you will observe your thoughts and emotions and will be able to make amendments when needed. You can even change your mood by changing your thoughts.

You see, when anger takes hold of us, we can step back and realise that we're feeling angry. What does this mean? It means you're not just a collection of thoughts and feelings in your brain. In "Super Brain," we suggest that the real you is the self-aware you, the one observing those thoughts and feelings. By mastering how you deal with your thoughts and emotions, you can use your brain to its fullest. You can shape the world you want to live in and consciously choose how to live in it. The first big step is to understand that you're not just your brain's activity; you're its user, inventor, leader, and master. The trick is to always be aware of the thoughts and feelings your brain creates in response to the world around you. This is a kind of mindfulness that highlights your amazing gifts of self-awareness, choice, and free will. Dr Deepak Chopra explains it all so beautifully.

Children are not self-aware but are intrinsically motivated When you're intrinsically motivated, your work becomes a joy. Kids, for instance, work on tasks because they find them fun. As they get better at things, even more challenging tasks become pleasurable. That's when learning itself becomes its own reward. It's all about finding joy in what you do.

During your schooling and academic life, you were intrinsically motivated. And you were free to choose whatever you wanted to do. In freedom, nothing seemed impossible as there was no one in your way. You were at your creative best; only you didn't know the treasure hidden within you. You enjoyed the discoveries you made. You were the judge of your worth, and the aim is to discover infinite worth in yourself

You may have noticed that the recurring theme throughout your boarding school life was having fun and enjoying every moment. According to Deepak Chopra,   happiness often comes from external things, but joy is something different. Joy comes from within us. While happiness can be tied to our circumstances, joy is a state of simply being. True joy is rooted in our very essence. It's like the wisdom of the world tells us that boundless delight and bliss are at the core of reality itself, and therefore, within us too. This inner joy isn't dependent on outside factors; it's a lasting, inherent quality of our true selves. It's a part of who we are at the deepest level, unlike happiness, which can come and go with circumstances. "Joy originates from within; it is a state of being."

Though you were unaware of this, the freedom allowed you to be close to your true self, and you experienced joy. Whether people are aware or not, every human's core desire is to experience joy all his life, from birth to death. A baby wants nothing but joy and gives off nothing but joy in return. "We all seek happiness and joy, two similar but distinct experiences. As our awareness expands, we realise that our circumstances matter less. Our joy starts to shine through in all situations, unaffected by life's changes.

.

CHAPTER FOUR

TONIC OF LIFE

The tonic of life is fun and playfulness. You see, my child, daily fun is like a daily dose of life's energy. It brings laughter and keeps us moving forward. Those who don't find joy in each day might need to rethink things. Something might be amiss in their lives. This wisdom comes from George Matthew Adams, as Ashoke Agarwal mentions in his article "Why Fun is Must in Life."

Go down the memory lane of your childhood until you spend it in a boarding house and college hostels away from home, unbounded and free from any constraint. You will distinctly recall those days full of fun and playful ventures. Your minds constantly seek fun-filled moments, wanting nothing but to amuse yourself. This playfulness is essential to nature to all beings and is the tonic of life.

You know, David Graeber had a conversation with June Thunderstorm, and she told him, "All animals play, even ants." She was a professional gardener and had seen many instances of this in nature. Graeber goes on to mention that even evolutionary psychologists have noticed playfulness everywhere in nature, even in electrons. They wonder why fun is fun and question whether electrons "choose" their actions. It's a tough question to prove, but it makes sense to consider that some form of intentionality, experience, and freedom exists at every level of physical reality, as part of a materialist view of the world. That's the essence of what

Graeber discusses in his article titled "What's the Point If We Can't Have Fun."

Electrons move as if their actions respond to stimuli as if they are conscious of what is happening around them, just as humans or any other species are conscious and respond to touching something hot. or react according to their experience. Their actions are automatic. Not only the electrons but every part of the cosmos is conscious, and their activities are taken independently and based on their experiences and the moment's need. The purpose of all the parts of the universe is to save themselves and the universe from disintegrating. "The universe is full of interconnected parts. In our Solar System, countless large objects orbit the galactic centre for hundreds of millions of years, all discussed in Ethan Siegel's article "Why Do All The Planets Orbit In The Same Plane?"

In your free days of schooling, you were self-governed; there were no outward constraints; you yourself were responsible for your life and were free to think and act as you intended/desired in your experiences, fearlessly. When you had no social conditioning and no one controlled you,   There was no fear of failure. Then you were orbiting/behaving in the same plane the planets and electrons orbit or behave. Your behaviour was natural. As natural as the other parts of the universe are natural because your mind is free, and a free mind pursues fun. The fun comes when you intend to act without any constraints, take actions as you desire and are responsible for the consequences. Whether negative or positive, the consequences of your actions leave you with invaluable experiences, and you develop and evolve fast.

In contrast, everything changes when you come in contact with social life. You acquire knowledge from society and accept it as a reality without finding its truthfulness; gradually, your mind is conditioned with this worldly knowledge.   You had not the faintest idea how the conditioning happened, and this conditioned mind becomes your reality, an unreal reality and the cause of all troubles and chaos in life and the world.   It is a matter of great anguish that almost the whole world is a victim of social conditioning – a society whose mind is conditioned is not free to do things his way and misses the peace it wants. There cannot be peace and harmony in the world unless people are liberated from social conditions and conditionings. The only way to free oneself from the condition is to deny the things one sees. You deny it means doubting everything. When you doubt things, you want to know the reality the way you always doubted in your academic life and discuss or do an in-depth investigation to find the truth. The real fun of life is in doubting everything and exploring things thoroughly.

Before entering real life, you had the freedom to intend and think the way you desired based on your experiences and take action, which amused you, and you had fun in its entirety. Then you are naturally attentive to your heart which is perfectly aligned with cosmic consciousness. You were aligned with your heart's consciousness because you could have fun and act in whatever you thought fit. You had no doubts. Your heart never allowed you to be controlled by others and to accept instruction against your free will.

Playfulness is embedded in you and every part of the universe. What's the point if we can't have fun? Look around; you can find everylife enjoying playing. You will find even water, air, and light at play if you have a keen eye. You see, that's just how Mother Nature works. She flourishes when her children are playful and joyful. Wise mothers understand that joy comes from within and doesn't depend on external circumstances. Our ego and intellect have often led us away from this beautiful instinct in our search for logic. Thanks to our ego, we no longer pay attention to that very significant aspect of our inborn funny bones.

Let's see the fun-filled behaviours we observe in us and around us in nature. When you have the freedom, you intend to get fun out of your actions. Most often, you haven't gotten the desired result. That's why you often fail. But you undoubtedly gained experience from your failures, and you enjoyed your experience. Your experience was gratifying because you enjoyed the play of mind. Whether mental or physical, playing or actions are always gratifying, and gainful experiences are fun.

Altruism can be quite puzzling. David Graeber raises some interesting questions about it. Why would animals ever sacrifice their own well-being for others? Yet, they sometimes do. Take honeybees, for instance. When their hive is under attack, they form these intense defensive groups called 'hot defensive bee balls.' These bees literally risk their lives to protect the hive. It's a bit of a mystery because, if we try to explain it scientifically, we wonder what these kamikaze bees are trying to maximise. Their actions are quite extraordinary, and it's a fascinating topic, as Graeber points out.

Altruism is also an act without motivation, just as fun has no motives. You can observe lambs at play, birds hanging upside down, fish chasing each other for fun, and monkeys moving by hanging underneath branches and using their arms to swing between each support. They all are playing just for fun without any motivation. So are humans. If you ask children why they are playing, the answer would be "just for fun". Our ego's unrealistic craving for more and evermore disengaged us from enjoying the fun of life. Your instinct for play and fun never dies, and you often have family and friends get-togethers for fun. Though not with that freedom kids have or you had during your educational journey.

You know, child, life teaches us a valuable lesson: every second spent in unhappiness is second wasted, never to be reclaimed. People today often chase happiness through various means like weight loss, new clothes, or seeking popularity on social media. But they sometimes forget the most important part of being happy –

having fun along the way.

It might be a pleasant surprise for most to know that fun and laughter heal. Laughter is one of the most potent medicines. It brings people together and brings positive changes to your body and emotions. It boosts your immune system, lifts your mood, eases pain, and shields you from stress's harmful effects. Nothing works as swiftly and consistently as a good laugh to restore balance to your mind and body. Humour has a way of lightening your load, sparking hope, fostering connections, and keeping you centred, attentive, and lively. It even helps you let go of anger and forgive more easily.

You see, our bodies produce natural chemicals called endorphins to help us deal with pain and stress. They're often called "feel-good" chemicals because they relieve pain and boost happiness. Doctors sometimes prescribe opioid drugs to patients in pain because they trigger the release of these endorphins. It's like a quick path to pain relief and a sense of well-being. But here's the catch: when the effect wears off, some folks may want that good feeling back, and that's when the road to potential addiction can begin. However, there are cases where people find pain relief without opioids. Norman Cousins' book, "An Anatomy of Illness As Perceived by Patient," is a fine example of this.

Let me tell you about Norman Cousins, a political journalist and activist. In the 1970s, he received a bleak diagnosis: ankylosing spondylitis. The doctors said he had a one in five hundred chance of recovery, and he was looking at a life of severe physical disability. But Cousins wasn't one to give up easily. He delved into brain chemistry and believed that laughter therapy could help him. Following his doctor's advice, he took high doses of Vitamin C, maintained a healthy diet, and watched funny movies every day. It might sound astonishing, but he began to get better. In the end, Cousins made a full recovery from his illness. He was so inspired by his experience that he wrote a memoir called "Anatomy of an

Illness" to encourage other patients to take an active role in their treatment. Today, his story is celebrated as a case study of the healing power of joy and laughter therapy.

You know,   laughter is more than just a burst of joy. It's like adding rich patterns to the tapestry of our daily lives. When we laugh in response to funny moments, it's not as simple as it seems. It actually involves quite a bit of brain power because it activates various parts of the brain that handle movement, emotions, thinking, and social interactions. So, those giggles and guffaws are doing more for us than we might think!

Your academic life was vastly different from present-day situations. In school and college, you had the freedom to think and do as you desired, and the desire was to do something unique to help you distinguish yourself from others. Constantly round the clock, your mind is busy thinking to make your days full of fun and laughter. That was possible because you were free and fearless and had a curious mind – a mind you were born with. You had no worries or anxiety and enjoyed the best health and happiness. Now you are deprived of your scientific mind, which sought reason and explanation. To enjoy the fun of life, you need to salvage your lost scientific mind. I wrote the next chapter titled The Scientific Mind in hopes that it will help you retrieve your fun moments.

The tonic of life is fun and playfulness. You see, my child, daily fun is like a daily dose of life's energy. It brings laughter and keeps us moving forward. Those who don't find joy in each day might need to rethink things. Something might be amiss in their lives. This wisdom comes from George Matthew Adams, as Ashoke Agarwal mentions in his article "Why Fun is Must in Life."

Go down the memory lane of your childhood until you spend it in a boarding house and college hostels away from home, unbounded and free from any constraint. You will distinctly recall those days full of fun and playful ventures. Your minds constantly seek fun-filled moments, wanting nothing but to amuse yourself. This playfulness is essential to nature to all beings and is the tonic of life.

You know, David Graeber had a conversation with June Thunderstorm, and she told him, "All animals play, even ants." She was a professional gardener and had seen many instances of this in nature. Graeber goes on to mention that even evolutionary psychologists have noticed playfulness everywhere in nature, even in electrons. They wonder why fun is fun and question whether electrons "choose" their actions. It's a tough question to prove, but it makes sense to consider that some form of intentionality, experience, and freedom exists at every level of physical reality, as part of a materialist view of the world. That's the essence of what Graeber discusses in his article titled "What's the Point If We Can't Have Fun."

Electrons move as if their actions respond to stimuli as if they are conscious of what is happening around them, just as humans or any other species are conscious and respond to touching something hot. or react according to their experience. Their actions are automatic. Not only the electrons but every part of the cosmos is conscious, and their activities are taken independently and based on their experiences and the moment's need. The purpose of all the parts of the universe is to save themselves and the universe from disintegrating. "The universe is full of interconnected parts. In our Solar System, countless large objects orbit the galactic centre for hundreds of millions of years, all discussed in Ethan Siegel's article "Why Do All The Planets Orbit In The Same Plane?"

In your free days of schooling, you were self-governed; there were no outward constraints; you yourself were responsible for your life and were free to think and act as you intended/desired in your experiences, fearlessly. When you had no social conditioning and no one controlled you,   There was no fear of failure. Then you were orbiting/behaving in the same plane the planets and electrons orbit or behave. Your behaviour was natural. As natural as the other parts of the universe are natural because your mind is free, and a free mind pursues fun. The fun comes when you intend to act without any constraints, take actions as you desire and are responsible for the consequences. Whether negative or positive, the consequences of your actions leave you with invaluable experiences, and you develop and evolve fast.

In contrast, everything changes when you come in contact with social life. You acquire knowledge from society and accept it as a reality without finding its truthfulness; gradually, your mind is conditioned with this worldly knowledge.   You had not the faintest idea how the conditioning happened, and this conditioned mind becomes your reality, an unreal reality and the cause of all troubles and chaos in life and the world.   It is a matter of great anguish that almost the whole world is a victim of social conditioning – a society whose mind is conditioned is not free to do things his way and misses the peace it wants. There cannot be peace and harmony in the world unless people are liberated from social conditions and conditionings. The only way to free oneself from the condition is to deny the things one sees. You deny it means doubting everything. When you doubt things, you want to know the reality the way you always doubted in your academic life and discuss or do an in-depth investigation to find the truth. The real fun of life is in doubting everything and exploring things thoroughly.

Before entering real life, you had the freedom to intend and think the way you desired based on your experiences and take

action, which amused you, and you had fun in its entirety. Then you are naturally attentive to your heart which is perfectly aligned with cosmic consciousness. You were aligned with your heart's consciousness because you could have fun and act in whatever you thought fit. You had no doubts. Your heart never allowed you to be controlled by others and to accept instruction against your free will.

Playfulness is embedded in you and every part of the universe. What's the point if we can't have fun? Look around; you can find everylife enjoying playing. You will find even water, air, and light at play if you have a keen eye. You see, that's just how Mother Nature works. She flourishes when her children are playful and joyful. Wise mothers understand that joy comes from within and doesn't depend on external circumstances. Our ego and intellect have often led us away from this beautiful instinct in our search for logic. Thanks to our ego, we no longer pay attention to that very significant aspect of our inborn funny bones.

Let's see the fun-filled behaviours we observe in us and around us in nature. When you have the freedom, you intend to get fun out of your actions. Most often, you haven't gotten the desired result. That's why you often fail. But you undoubtedly gained experience from your failures, and you enjoyed your experience. Your experience was gratifying because you enjoyed the play of mind. Whether mental or physical, playing or actions are always gratifying, and gainful experiences are fun.

Altruism can be quite puzzling. David Graeber raises some interesting questions about it. Why would animals ever sacrifice their own well-being for others? Yet, they sometimes do. Take honeybees, for instance. When their hive is under attack, they form these intense defensive groups called 'hot defensive bee balls.' These bees literally risk their lives to protect the hive. It's a bit of a mystery because, if we try to explain it scientifically, we wonder what these kamikaze bees are trying to maximise. Their actions are quite extraordinary, and it's a fascinating topic, as Graeber points

out.

Altruism is also an act without motivation, just as fun has no motives. You can observe lambs at play, birds hanging upside down, fish chasing each other for fun, and monkeys moving by hanging underneath branches and using their arms to swing between each support. They all are playing just for fun without any motivation. So are humans. If you ask children why they are playing, the answer would be "just for fun". Our ego's unrealistic craving for more and evermore disengaged us from enjoying the fun of life. Your instinct for play and fun never dies, and you often have family and friends get-togethers for fun. Though not with that freedom kids have or you had during your educational journey.

You know, child, life teaches us a valuable lesson: every second spent in unhappiness is second wasted, never to be reclaimed. People today often chase happiness through various means like weight loss, new clothes, or seeking popularity on social media. But they sometimes forget the most important part of being happy – having fun along the way.

It might be a pleasant surprise for most to know that fun and laughter heal. Laughter is one of the most potent medicines. It brings people together and brings positive changes to your body and emotions. It boosts your immune system, lifts your mood, eases pain, and shields you from stress's harmful effects. Nothing works as swiftly and consistently as a good laugh to restore balance to your mind and body. Humour has a way of lightening your load, sparking hope, fostering connections, and keeping you centred, attentive, and lively. It even helps you let go of anger and forgive more easily.

You see, our bodies produce natural chemicals called endorphins to help us deal with pain and stress. They're often called "feel-good" chemicals because they relieve pain and boost happiness. Doctors sometimes prescribe opioid drugs to patients

in pain because they trigger the release of these endorphins. It's like a quick path to pain relief and a sense of well-being. But here's the catch: when the effect wears off, some folks may want that good feeling back, and that's when the road to potential addiction can begin. However, there are cases where people find pain relief without opioids. Norman Cousins' book, "An Anatomy of Illness As Perceived by Patient," is a fine example of this.

Let me tell you about Norman Cousins, a political journalist and activist. In the 1970s, he received a bleak diagnosis: ankylosing spondylitis. The doctors said he had a one in five hundred chance of recovery, and he was looking at a life of severe physical disability. But Cousins wasn't one to give up easily. He delved into brain chemistry and believed that laughter therapy could help him. Following his doctor's advice, he took high doses of Vitamin C, maintained a healthy diet, and watched funny movies every day. It might sound astonishing, but he began to get better. In the end, Cousins made a full recovery from his illness. He was so inspired by his experience that he wrote a memoir called "Anatomy of an Illness" to encourage other patients to take an active role in their treatment. Today, his story is celebrated as a case study of the healing power of joy and laughter therapy.

You know,   laughter is more than just a burst of joy. It's like adding rich patterns to the tapestry of our daily lives. When we laugh in response to funny moments, it's not as simple as it seems. It actually involves quite a bit of brain power because it activates various parts of the brain that handle movement, emotions, thinking, and social interactions. So, those giggles and guffaws are doing more for us than we might think!

Your academic life was vastly different from present-day situations. In school and college, you had the freedom to think and do as you desired, and the desire was to do something unique to help you distinguish yourself from others. Constantly round the

clock, your mind is busy thinking to make your days full of fun and laughter. That was possible because you were free and fearless and had a curious mind – a mind you were born with. You had no worries or anxiety and enjoyed the best health and happiness. Now you are deprived of your scientific mind, which sought reason and explanation. To enjoy the fun of life, you need to salvage your lost scientific mind. I wrote the next chapter titled The Scientific Mind in hopes that it will help you retrieve your fun moments.

The tonic of life is fun and playfulness. You see, my child, daily fun is like a daily dose of life's energy. It brings laughter and keeps us moving forward. Those who don't find joy in each day might need to rethink things. Something might be amiss in their lives. This wisdom comes from George Matthew Adams, as Ashoke Agarwal mentions in his article "Why Fun is Must in Life."

Go down the memory lane of your childhood until you spend it in a boarding house and college hostels away from home, unbounded and free from any constraint. You will distinctly recall those days full of fun and playful ventures. Your minds constantly seek fun-filled moments, wanting nothing but to amuse yourself. This playfulness is essential to nature to all beings and is the tonic of life.

You know, David Graeber had a conversation with June Thunderstorm, and she told him, "All animals play, even ants." She was a professional gardener and had seen many instances of this in nature. Graeber goes on to mention that even evolutionary psychologists have noticed playfulness everywhere in nature, even in electrons. They wonder why fun is fun and question whether electrons "choose" their actions. It's a tough question to prove, but it makes sense to consider that some form of intentionality, experience, and freedom exists at every level of physical reality, as

part of a materialist view of the world. That's the essence of what Graeber discusses in his article titled "What's the Point If We Can't Have Fun."

Electrons move as if their actions respond to stimuli as if they are conscious of what is happening around them, just as humans or any other species are conscious and respond to touching something hot. or react according to their experience. Their actions are automatic. Not only the electrons but every part of the cosmos is conscious, and their activities are taken independently and based on their experiences and the moment's need. The purpose of all the parts of the universe is to save themselves and the universe from disintegrating. "The universe is full of interconnected parts. In our Solar System, countless large objects orbit the galactic centre for hundreds of millions of years, all discussed in Ethan Siegel's article "Why Do All The Planets Orbit In The Same Plane?"

In your free days of schooling, you were self-governed; there were no outward constraints; you yourself were responsible for your life and were free to think and act as you intended/desired in your experiences, fearlessly. When you had no social conditioning and no one controlled you,   There was no fear of failure. Then you were orbiting/behaving in the same plane the planets and electrons orbit or behave. Your behaviour was natural. As natural as the other parts of the universe are natural because your mind is free, and a free mind pursues fun. The fun comes when you intend to act without any constraints, take actions as you desire and are responsible for the consequences. Whether negative or positive, the consequences of your actions leave you with invaluable experiences, and you develop and evolve fast.

In contrast, everything changes when you come in contact with social life. You acquire knowledge from society and accept it as a reality without finding its truthfulness; gradually, your mind is conditioned with this worldly knowledge.   You had not the

faintest idea how the conditioning happened, and this conditioned mind becomes your reality, an unreal reality and the cause of all troubles and chaos in life and the world.   It is a matter of great anguish that almost the whole world is a victim of social conditioning – a society whose mind is conditioned is not free to do things his way and misses the peace it wants. There cannot be peace and harmony in the world unless people are liberated from social conditions and conditionings. The only way to free oneself from the condition is to deny the things one sees. You deny it means doubting everything. When you doubt things, you want to know the reality the way you always doubted in your academic life and discuss or do an in-depth investigation to find the truth. The real fun of life is in doubting everything and exploring things thoroughly.

Before entering real life, you had the freedom to intend and think the way you desired based on your experiences and take action, which amused you, and you had fun in its entirety. Then you are naturally attentive to your heart which is perfectly aligned with cosmic consciousness. You were aligned with your heart's consciousness because you could have fun and act in whatever you thought fit. You had no doubts. Your heart never allowed you to be controlled by others and to accept instruction against your free will.

Playfulness is embedded in you and every part of the universe. What's the point if we can't have fun? Look around; you can find everylife enjoying playing. You will find even water, air, and light at play if you have a keen eye. You see, that's just how Mother Nature works. She flourishes when her children are playful and joyful. Wise mothers understand that joy comes from within and doesn't depend on external circumstances. Our ego and intellect have often led us away from this beautiful instinct in our search for logic. Thanks to our ego, we no longer pay attention to that very significant aspect of our inborn funny bones.

Let's see the fun-filled behaviours we observe in us and around us in nature. When you have the freedom, you intend to get fun out of your actions. Most often, you haven't gotten the desired result. That's why you often fail. But you undoubtedly gained experience from your failures, and you enjoyed your experience. Your experience was gratifying because you enjoyed the play of mind. Whether mental or physical, playing or actions are always gratifying, and gainful experiences are fun.

Altruism can be quite puzzling. David Graeber raises some interesting questions about it. Why would animals ever sacrifice their own well-being for others? Yet, they sometimes do. Take honeybees, for instance. When their hive is under attack, they form these intense defensive groups called 'hot defensive bee balls.' These bees literally risk their lives to protect the hive. It's a bit of a mystery because, if we try to explain it scientifically, we wonder what these kamikaze bees are trying to maximise. Their actions are quite extraordinary, and it's a fascinating topic, as Graeber points out.

Altruism is also an act without motivation, just as fun has no motives. You can observe lambs at play, birds hanging upside down, fish chasing each other for fun, and monkeys moving by hanging underneath branches and using their arms to swing between each support. They all are playing just for fun without any motivation. So are humans. If you ask children why they are playing, the answer would be "just for fun". Our ego's unrealistic craving for more and evermore disengaged us from enjoying the fun of life. Your instinct for play and fun never dies, and you often have family and friends get-togethers for fun. Though not with that freedom kids have or you had during your educational journey.

You know, child, life teaches us a valuable lesson: every second spent in unhappiness is second wasted, never to be reclaimed. People today often chase happiness through various means like

weight loss, new clothes, or seeking popularity on social media. But they sometimes forget the most important part of being happy – having fun along the way.

It might be a pleasant surprise for most to know that fun and laughter heal. Laughter is one of the most potent medicines. It brings people together and brings positive changes to your body and emotions. It boosts your immune system, lifts your mood, eases pain, and shields you from stress's harmful effects. Nothing works as swiftly and consistently as a good laugh to restore balance to your mind and body. Humour has a way of lightening your load, sparking hope, fostering connections, and keeping you centred, attentive, and lively. It even helps you let go of anger and forgive more easily.

You see, our bodies produce natural chemicals called endorphins to help us deal with pain and stress. They're often called "feel-good" chemicals because they relieve pain and boost happiness. Doctors sometimes prescribe opioid drugs to patients in pain because they trigger the release of these endorphins. It's like a quick path to pain relief and a sense of well-being. But here's the catch: when the effect wears off, some folks may want that good feeling back, and that's when the road to potential addiction can begin. However, there are cases where people find pain relief without opioids. Norman Cousins' book, "An Anatomy of Illness As Perceived by Patient," is a fine example of this.

Let me tell you about Norman Cousins, a political journalist and activist. In the 1970s, he received a bleak diagnosis: ankylosing spondylitis. The doctors said he had a one in five hundred chance of recovery, and he was looking at a life of severe physical disability. But Cousins wasn't one to give up easily. He delved into brain chemistry and believed that laughter therapy could help him. Following his doctor's advice, he took high doses of Vitamin C, maintained a healthy diet, and watched funny movies every day. It might sound astonishing, but he began to get better. In the end,

Cousins made a full recovery from his illness. He was so inspired by his experience that he wrote a memoir called "Anatomy of an Illness" to encourage other patients to take an active role in their treatment. Today, his story is celebrated as a case study of the healing power of joy and laughter therapy.

You know,   laughter is more than just a burst of joy. It's like adding rich patterns to the tapestry of our daily lives. When we laugh in response to funny moments, it's not as simple as it seems. It actually involves quite a bit of brain power because it activates various parts of the brain that handle movement, emotions, thinking, and social interactions. So, those giggles and guffaws are doing more for us than we might think!

Your academic life was vastly different from present-day situations. In school and college, you had the freedom to think and do as you desired, and the desire was to do something unique to help you distinguish yourself from others. Constantly round the clock, your mind is busy thinking to make your days full of fun and laughter. That was possible because you were free and fearless and had a curious mind – a mind you were born with. You had no worries or anxiety and enjoyed the best health and happiness. Now you are deprived of your scientific mind, which sought reason and explanation. To enjoy the fun of life, you need to salvage your lost scientific mind. I wrote the next chapter titled The Scientific Mind in hopes that it will help you retrieve your fun moments.

The tonic of life is fun and playfulness. You see, my child, daily fun is like a daily dose of life's energy. It brings laughter and keeps us moving forward. Those who don't find joy in each day might need to rethink things. Something might be amiss in their lives. This wisdom comes from George Matthew Adams, as Ashoke Agarwal mentions in his article "Why Fun is Must in Life."

Go down the memory lane of your childhood until you spend it in a boarding house and college hostels away from home, unbounded and free from any constraint. You will distinctly recall those days full of fun and playful ventures. Your minds constantly seek fun-filled moments, wanting nothing but to amuse yourself. This playfulness is essential to nature to all beings and is the tonic of life.

You know, David Graeber had a conversation with June Thunderstorm, and she told him, "All animals play, even ants." She was a professional gardener and had seen many instances of this in nature. Graeber goes on to mention that even evolutionary psychologists have noticed playfulness everywhere in nature, even in electrons. They wonder why fun is fun and question whether electrons "choose" their actions. It's a tough question to prove, but it makes sense to consider that some form of intentionality, experience, and freedom exists at every level of physical reality, as part of a materialist view of the world. That's the essence of what Graeber discusses in his article titled "What's the Point If We Can't Have Fun."

Electrons move as if their actions respond to stimuli as if they are conscious of what is happening around them, just as humans or any other species are conscious and respond to touching something hot. or react according to their experience. Their actions are automatic. Not only the electrons but every part of the cosmos is conscious, and their activities are taken independently and based on their experiences and the moment's need. The purpose of all the parts of the universe is to save themselves and the universe from disintegrating. "The universe is full of interconnected parts. In our Solar System, countless large objects orbit the galactic centre for hundreds of millions of years, all discussed in Ethan Siegel's article "Why Do All The Planets Orbit In The Same Plane?"

In your free days of schooling, you were self-governed; there were no outward constraints; you yourself were responsible for your life and were free to think and act as you intended/desired in your experiences, fearlessly. When you had no social conditioning and no one controlled you,   There was no fear of failure. Then you were orbiting/behaving in the same plane the planets and electrons orbit or behave. Your behaviour was natural. As natural as the other parts of the universe are natural because your mind is free, and a free mind pursues fun. The fun comes when you intend to act without any constraints, take actions as you desire and are responsible for the consequences. Whether negative or positive, the consequences of your actions leave you with invaluable experiences, and you develop and evolve fast.

In contrast, everything changes when you come in contact with social life. You acquire knowledge from society and accept it as a reality without finding its truthfulness; gradually, your mind is conditioned with this worldly knowledge.   You had not the faintest idea how the conditioning happened, and this conditioned mind becomes your reality, an unreal reality and the cause of all troubles and chaos in life and the world.   It is a matter of great anguish that almost the whole world is a victim of social conditioning – a society whose mind is conditioned is not free to do things his way and misses the peace it wants. There cannot be peace and harmony in the world unless people are liberated from social conditions and conditionings. The only way to free oneself from the condition is to deny the things one sees. You deny it means doubting everything. When you doubt things, you want to know the reality the way you always doubted in your academic life and discuss or do an in-depth investigation to find the truth. The real fun of life is in doubting everything and exploring things thoroughly.

Before entering real life, you had the freedom to intend and think the way you desired based on your experiences and take

action, which amused you, and you had fun in its entirety. Then you are naturally attentive to your heart which is perfectly aligned with cosmic consciousness. You were aligned with your heart's consciousness because you could have fun and act in whatever you thought fit. You had no doubts. Your heart never allowed you to be controlled by others and to accept instruction against your free will.

Playfulness is embedded in you and every part of the universe. What's the point if we can't have fun? Look around; you can find everylife enjoying playing. You will find even water, air, and light at play if you have a keen eye. You see, that's just how Mother Nature works. She flourishes when her children are playful and joyful. Wise mothers understand that joy comes from within and doesn't depend on external circumstances. Our ego and intellect have often led us away from this beautiful instinct in our search for logic. Thanks to our ego, we no longer pay attention to that very significant aspect of our inborn funny bones.

Let's see the fun-filled behaviours we observe in us and around us in nature. When you have the freedom, you intend to get fun out of your actions. Most often, you haven't gotten the desired result. That's why you often fail. But you undoubtedly gained experience from your failures, and you enjoyed your experience. Your experience was gratifying because you enjoyed the play of mind. Whether mental or physical, playing or actions are always gratifying, and gainful experiences are fun.

Altruism can be quite puzzling. David Graeber raises some interesting questions about it. Why would animals ever sacrifice their own well-being for others? Yet, they sometimes do. Take honeybees, for instance. When their hive is under attack, they form these intense defensive groups called 'hot defensive bee balls.' These bees literally risk their lives to protect the hive. It's a bit of a mystery because, if we try to explain it scientifically, we wonder what these kamikaze bees are trying to maximise. Their actions are quite extraordinary, and it's a fascinating topic, as Graeber points

out.

Altruism is also an act without motivation, just as fun has no motives. You can observe lambs at play, birds hanging upside down, fish chasing each other for fun, and monkeys moving by hanging underneath branches and using their arms to swing between each support. They all are playing just for fun without any motivation. So are humans. If you ask children why they are playing, the answer would be "just for fun". Our ego's unrealistic craving for more and evermore disengaged us from enjoying the fun of life. Your instinct for play and fun never dies, and you often have family and friends get-togethers for fun. Though not with that freedom kids have or you had during your educational journey.

You know, child, life teaches us a valuable lesson: every second spent in unhappiness is second wasted, never to be reclaimed. People today often chase happiness through various means like weight loss, new clothes, or seeking popularity on social media. But they sometimes forget the most important part of being happy – having fun along the way.

It might be a pleasant surprise for most to know that fun and laughter heal. Laughter is one of the most potent medicines. It brings people together and brings positive changes to your body and emotions. It boosts your immune system, lifts your mood, eases pain, and shields you from stress's harmful effects. Nothing works as swiftly and consistently as a good laugh to restore balance to your mind and body. Humour has a way of lightening your load, sparking hope, fostering connections, and keeping you centred, attentive, and lively. It even helps you let go of anger and forgive more easily.

You see, our bodies produce natural chemicals called endorphins to help us deal with pain and stress. They're often called "feel-good" chemicals because they relieve pain and boost happiness. Doctors sometimes prescribe opioid drugs to patients

in pain because they trigger the release of these endorphins. It's like a quick path to pain relief and a sense of well-being. But here's the catch: when the effect wears off, some folks may want that good feeling back, and that's when the road to potential addiction can begin. However, there are cases where people find pain relief without opioids. Norman Cousins' book, "An Anatomy of Illness As Perceived by Patient," is a fine example of this.

Let me tell you about Norman Cousins, a political journalist and activist. In the 1970s, he received a bleak diagnosis: ankylosing spondylitis. The doctors said he had a one in five hundred chance of recovery, and he was looking at a life of severe physical disability. But Cousins wasn't one to give up easily. He delved into brain chemistry and believed that laughter therapy could help him. Following his doctor's advice, he took high doses of Vitamin C, maintained a healthy diet, and watched funny movies every day. It might sound astonishing, but he began to get better. In the end, Cousins made a full recovery from his illness. He was so inspired by his experience that he wrote a memoir called "Anatomy of an Illness" to encourage other patients to take an active role in their treatment. Today, his story is celebrated as a case study of the healing power of joy and laughter therapy.

You know,   laughter is more than just a burst of joy. It's like adding rich patterns to the tapestry of our daily lives. When we laugh in response to funny moments, it's not as simple as it seems. It actually involves quite a bit of brain power because it activates various parts of the brain that handle movement, emotions, thinking, and social interactions. So, those giggles and guffaws are doing more for us than we might think!

Your academic life was vastly different from present-day situations. In school and college, you had the freedom to think and do as you desired, and the desire was to do something unique to help you distinguish yourself from others. Constantly round the

clock, your mind is busy thinking to make your days full of fun and laughter. That was possible because you were free and fearless and had a curious mind – a mind you were born with. You had no worries or anxiety and enjoyed the best health and happiness. Now you are deprived of your scientific mind, which sought reason and explanation. To enjoy the fun of life, you need to salvage your lost scientific mind. I wrote the next chapter titled The Scientific Mind in hopes that it will help you retrieve your fun moments.

The tonic of life is fun and playfulness. You see, my child, daily fun is like a daily dose of life's energy. It brings laughter and keeps us moving forward. Those who don't find joy in each day might need to rethink things. Something might be amiss in their lives. This wisdom comes from George Matthew Adams, as Ashoke Agarwal mentions in his article "Why Fun is Must in Life."

Go down the memory lane of your childhood until you spend it in a boarding house and college hostels away from home, unbounded and free from any constraint. You will distinctly recall those days full of fun and playful ventures. Your minds constantly seek fun-filled moments, wanting nothing but to amuse yourself. This playfulness is essential to nature to all beings and is the tonic of life.

You know, David Graeber had a conversation with June Thunderstorm, and she told him, "All animals play, even ants." She was a professional gardener and had seen many instances of this in nature. Graeber goes on to mention that even evolutionary psychologists have noticed playfulness everywhere in nature, even in electrons. They wonder why fun is fun and question whether electrons "choose" their actions. It's a tough question to prove, but it makes sense to consider that some form of intentionality, experience, and freedom exists at every level of physical reality, as

part of a materialist view of the world. That's the essence of what Graeber discusses in his article titled "What's the Point If We Can't Have Fun."

Electrons move as if their actions respond to stimuli as if they are conscious of what is happening around them, just as humans or any other species are conscious and respond to touching something hot. or react according to their experience. Their actions are automatic. Not only the electrons but every part of the cosmos is conscious, and their activities are taken independently and based on their experiences and the moment's need. The purpose of all the parts of the universe is to save themselves and the universe from disintegrating. "The universe is full of interconnected parts. In our Solar System, countless large objects orbit the galactic centre for hundreds of millions of years, all discussed in Ethan Siegel's article "Why Do All The Planets Orbit In The Same Plane?"

In your free days of schooling, you were self-governed; there were no outward constraints; you yourself were responsible for your life and were free to think and act as you intended/desired in your experiences, fearlessly. When you had no social conditioning and no one controlled you,   There was no fear of failure. Then you were orbiting/behaving in the same plane the planets and electrons orbit or behave. Your behaviour was natural. As natural as the other parts of the universe are natural because your mind is free, and a free mind pursues fun. The fun comes when you intend to act without any constraints, take actions as you desire and are responsible for the consequences. Whether negative or positive, the consequences of your actions leave you with invaluable experiences, and you develop and evolve fast.

In contrast, everything changes when you come in contact with social life. You acquire knowledge from society and accept it as a reality without finding its truthfulness; gradually, your mind is conditioned with this worldly knowledge.   You had not the

faintest idea how the conditioning happened, and this conditioned mind becomes your reality, an unreal reality and the cause of all troubles and chaos in life and the world.   It is a matter of great anguish that almost the whole world is a victim of social conditioning – a society whose mind is conditioned is not free to do things his way and misses the peace it wants. There cannot be peace and harmony in the world unless people are liberated from social conditions and conditionings. The only way to free oneself from the condition is to deny the things one sees. You deny it means doubting everything. When you doubt things, you want to know the reality the way you always doubted in your academic life and discuss or do an in-depth investigation to find the truth. The real fun of life is in doubting everything and exploring things thoroughly.

Before entering real life, you had the freedom to intend and think the way you desired based on your experiences and take action, which amused you, and you had fun in its entirety. Then you are naturally attentive to your heart which is perfectly aligned with cosmic consciousness. You were aligned with your heart's consciousness because you could have fun and act in whatever you thought fit. You had no doubts. Your heart never allowed you to be controlled by others and to accept instruction against your free will.

Playfulness is embedded in you and every part of the universe. What's the point if we can't have fun? Look around; you can find everylife enjoying playing. You will find even water, air, and light at play if you have a keen eye. You see, that's just how Mother Nature works. She flourishes when her children are playful and joyful. Wise mothers understand that joy comes from within and doesn't depend on external circumstances. Our ego and intellect have often led us away from this beautiful instinct in our search for logic. Thanks to our ego, we no longer pay attention to that very significant aspect of our inborn funny bones.

Let's see the fun-filled behaviours we observe in us and around us in nature. When you have the freedom, you intend to get fun out of your actions. Most often, you haven't gotten the desired result. That's why you often fail. But you undoubtedly gained experience from your failures, and you enjoyed your experience. Your experience was gratifying because you enjoyed the play of mind. Whether mental or physical, playing or actions are always gratifying, and gainful experiences are fun.

Altruism can be quite puzzling. David Graeber raises some interesting questions about it. Why would animals ever sacrifice their own well-being for others? Yet, they sometimes do. Take honeybees, for instance. When their hive is under attack, they form these intense defensive groups called 'hot defensive bee balls.' These bees literally risk their lives to protect the hive. It's a bit of a mystery because, if we try to explain it scientifically, we wonder what these kamikaze bees are trying to maximise. Their actions are quite extraordinary, and it's a fascinating topic, as Graeber points out.

Altruism is also an act without motivation, just as fun has no motives. You can observe lambs at play, birds hanging upside down, fish chasing each other for fun, and monkeys moving by hanging underneath branches and using their arms to swing between each support. They all are playing just for fun without any motivation. So are humans. If you ask children why they are playing, the answer would be "just for fun". Our ego's unrealistic craving for more and evermore disengaged us from enjoying the fun of life. Your instinct for play and fun never dies, and you often have family and friends get-togethers for fun. Though not with that freedom kids have or you had during your educational journey.

You know, child, life teaches us a valuable lesson: every second spent in unhappiness is second wasted, never to be reclaimed. People today often chase happiness through various means like

weight loss, new clothes, or seeking popularity on social media. But they sometimes forget the most important part of being happy – having fun along the way.

It might be a pleasant surprise for most to know that fun and laughter heal. Laughter is one of the most potent medicines. It brings people together and brings positive changes to your body and emotions. It boosts your immune system, lifts your mood, eases pain, and shields you from stress's harmful effects. Nothing works as swiftly and consistently as a good laugh to restore balance to your mind and body. Humour has a way of lightening your load, sparking hope, fostering connections, and keeping you centred, attentive, and lively. It even helps you let go of anger and forgive more easily.

You see, our bodies produce natural chemicals called endorphins to help us deal with pain and stress. They're often called "feel-good" chemicals because they relieve pain and boost happiness. Doctors sometimes prescribe opioid drugs to patients in pain because they trigger the release of these endorphins. It's like a quick path to pain relief and a sense of well-being. But here's the catch: when the effect wears off, some folks may want that good feeling back, and that's when the road to potential addiction can begin. However, there are cases where people find pain relief without opioids. Norman Cousins' book, "An Anatomy of Illness As Perceived by Patient," is a fine example of this.

Let me tell you about Norman Cousins, a political journalist and activist. In the 1970s, he received a bleak diagnosis: ankylosing spondylitis. The doctors said he had a one in five hundred chance of recovery, and he was looking at a life of severe physical disability. But Cousins wasn't one to give up easily. He delved into brain chemistry and believed that laughter therapy could help him. Following his doctor's advice, he took high doses of Vitamin C, maintained a healthy diet, and watched funny movies every day. It might sound astonishing, but he began to get better. In the end,

Cousins made a full recovery from his illness. He was so inspired by his experience that he wrote a memoir called "Anatomy of an Illness" to encourage other patients to take an active role in their treatment. Today, his story is celebrated as a case study of the healing power of joy and laughter therapy.

You know,   laughter is more than just a burst of joy. It's like adding rich patterns to the tapestry of our daily lives. When we laugh in response to funny moments, it's not as simple as it seems. It actually involves quite a bit of brain power because it activates various parts of the brain that handle movement, emotions, thinking, and social interactions. So, those giggles and guffaws are doing more for us than we might think!

Your academic life was vastly different from present-day situations. In school and college, you had the freedom to think and do as you desired, and the desire was to do something unique to help you distinguish yourself from others. Constantly round the clock, your mind is busy thinking to make your days full of fun and laughter. That was possible because you were free and fearless and had a curious mind – a mind you were born with. You had no worries or anxiety and enjoyed the best health and happiness. Now you are deprived of your scientific mind, which sought reason and explanation. To enjoy the fun of life, you need to salvage your lost scientific mind. I wrote the next chapter titled The Scientific Mind in hopes that it will help you retrieve your fun moments.

The tonic of life is fun and playfulness. You see, my child, daily fun is like a daily dose of life's energy. It brings laughter and keeps us moving forward. Those who don't find joy in each day might need to rethink things. Something might be amiss in their lives. This wisdom comes from George Matthew Adams, as Ashoke Agarwal mentions in his article "Why Fun is Must in Life."

Go down the memory lane of your childhood until you spend it in a boarding house and college hostels away from home, unbounded and free from any constraint. You will distinctly recall those days full of fun and playful ventures. Your minds constantly seek fun-filled moments, wanting nothing but to amuse yourself. This playfulness is essential to nature to all beings and is the tonic of life.

You know, David Graeber had a conversation with June Thunderstorm, and she told him, "All animals play, even ants." She was a professional gardener and had seen many instances of this in nature. Graeber goes on to mention that even evolutionary psychologists have noticed playfulness everywhere in nature, even in electrons. They wonder why fun is fun and question whether electrons "choose" their actions. It's a tough question to prove, but it makes sense to consider that some form of intentionality, experience, and freedom exists at every level of physical reality, as part of a materialist view of the world. That's the essence of what Graeber discusses in his article titled "What's the Point If We Can't Have Fun."

Electrons move as if their actions respond to stimuli as if they are conscious of what is happening around them, just as humans or any other species are conscious and respond to touching something hot. or react according to their experience. Their actions are automatic. Not only the electrons but every part of the cosmos is conscious, and their activities are taken independently and based on their experiences and the moment's need. The purpose of all the parts of the universe is to save themselves and the universe from disintegrating. "The universe is full of interconnected parts. In our Solar System, countless large objects orbit the galactic centre for hundreds of millions of years, all discussed in Ethan Siegel's article "Why Do All The Planets Orbit In The Same Plane?"

In your free days of schooling, you were self-governed; there were no outward constraints; you yourself were responsible for your life and were free to think and act as you intended/desired in your experiences, fearlessly. When you had no social conditioning and no one controlled you,   There was no fear of failure. Then you were orbiting/behaving in the same plane the planets and electrons orbit or behave. Your behaviour was natural. As natural as the other parts of the universe are natural because your mind is free, and a free mind pursues fun. The fun comes when you intend to act without any constraints, take actions as you desire and are responsible for the consequences. Whether negative or positive, the consequences of your actions leave you with invaluable experiences, and you develop and evolve fast.

In contrast, everything changes when you come in contact with social life. You acquire knowledge from society and accept it as a reality without finding its truthfulness; gradually, your mind is conditioned with this worldly knowledge.   You had not the faintest idea how the conditioning happened, and this conditioned mind becomes your reality, an unreal reality and the cause of all troubles and chaos in life and the world.   It is a matter of great anguish that almost the whole world is a victim of social conditioning – a society whose mind is conditioned is not free to do things his way and misses the peace it wants. There cannot be peace and harmony in the world unless people are liberated from social conditions and conditionings. The only way to free oneself from the condition is to deny the things one sees. You deny it means doubting everything. When you doubt things, you want to know the reality the way you always doubted in your academic life and discuss or do an in-depth investigation to find the truth. The real fun of life is in doubting everything and exploring things thoroughly.

Before entering real life, you had the freedom to intend and think the way you desired based on your experiences and take

action, which amused you, and you had fun in its entirety. Then you are naturally attentive to your heart which is perfectly aligned with cosmic consciousness. You were aligned with your heart's consciousness because you could have fun and act in whatever you thought fit. You had no doubts. Your heart never allowed you to be controlled by others and to accept instruction against your free will.

Playfulness is embedded in you and every part of the universe. What's the point if we can't have fun? Look around; you can find everylife enjoying playing. You will find even water, air, and light at play if you have a keen eye. You see, that's just how Mother Nature works. She flourishes when her children are playful and joyful. Wise mothers understand that joy comes from within and doesn't depend on external circumstances. Our ego and intellect have often led us away from this beautiful instinct in our search for logic. Thanks to our ego, we no longer pay attention to that very significant aspect of our inborn funny bones.

Let's see the fun-filled behaviours we observe in us and around us in nature. When you have the freedom, you intend to get fun out of your actions. Most often, you haven't gotten the desired result. That's why you often fail. But you undoubtedly gained experience from your failures, and you enjoyed your experience. Your experience was gratifying because you enjoyed the play of mind. Whether mental or physical, playing or actions are always gratifying, and gainful experiences are fun.

Altruism can be quite puzzling. David Graeber raises some interesting questions about it. Why would animals ever sacrifice their own well-being for others? Yet, they sometimes do. Take honeybees, for instance. When their hive is under attack, they form these intense defensive groups called 'hot defensive bee balls.' These bees literally risk their lives to protect the hive. It's a bit of a mystery because, if we try to explain it scientifically, we wonder what these kamikaze bees are trying to maximise. Their actions are quite extraordinary, and it's a fascinating topic, as Graeber points

out.

Altruism is also an act without motivation, just as fun has no motives. You can observe lambs at play, birds hanging upside down, fish chasing each other for fun, and monkeys moving by hanging underneath branches and using their arms to swing between each support. They all are playing just for fun without any motivation. So are humans. If you ask children why they are playing, the answer would be "just for fun". Our ego's unrealistic craving for more and evermore disengaged us from enjoying the fun of life. Your instinct for play and fun never dies, and you often have family and friends get-togethers for fun. Though not with that freedom kids have or you had during your educational journey.

You know, child, life teaches us a valuable lesson: every second spent in unhappiness is second wasted, never to be reclaimed. People today often chase happiness through various means like weight loss, new clothes, or seeking popularity on social media. But they sometimes forget the most important part of being happy — having fun along the way.

It might be a pleasant surprise for most to know that fun and laughter heal. Laughter is one of the most potent medicines. It brings people together and brings positive changes to your body and emotions. It boosts your immune system, lifts your mood, eases pain, and shields you from stress's harmful effects. Nothing works as swiftly and consistently as a good laugh to restore balance to your mind and body. Humour has a way of lightening your load, sparking hope, fostering connections, and keeping you centred, attentive, and lively. It even helps you let go of anger and forgive more easily.

You see, our bodies produce natural chemicals called endorphins to help us deal with pain and stress. They're often called "feel-good" chemicals because they relieve pain and boost happiness. Doctors sometimes prescribe opioid drugs to patients

in pain because they trigger the release of these endorphins. It's like a quick path to pain relief and a sense of well-being. But here's the catch: when the effect wears off, some folks may want that good feeling back, and that's when the road to potential addiction can begin. However, there are cases where people find pain relief without opioids. Norman Cousins' book, "An Anatomy of Illness As Perceived by Patient," is a fine example of this.

Let me tell you about Norman Cousins, a political journalist and activist. In the 1970s, he received a bleak diagnosis: ankylosing spondylitis. The doctors said he had a one in five hundred chance of recovery, and he was looking at a life of severe physical disability. But Cousins wasn't one to give up easily. He delved into brain chemistry and believed that laughter therapy could help him. Following his doctor's advice, he took high doses of Vitamin C, maintained a healthy diet, and watched funny movies every day. It might sound astonishing, but he began to get better. In the end, Cousins made a full recovery from his illness. He was so inspired by his experience that he wrote a memoir called "Anatomy of an Illness" to encourage other patients to take an active role in their treatment. Today, his story is celebrated as a case study of the healing power of joy and laughter therapy.

You know,   laughter is more than just a burst of joy. It's like adding rich patterns to the tapestry of our daily lives. When we laugh in response to funny moments, it's not as simple as it seems. It actually involves quite a bit of brain power because it activates various parts of the brain that handle movement, emotions, thinking, and social interactions. So, those giggles and guffaws are doing more for us than we might think!

Your academic life was vastly different from present-day situations. In school and college, you had the freedom to think and do as you desired, and the desire was to do something unique to help you distinguish yourself from others. Constantly round the

clock, your mind is busy thinking to make your days full of fun and laughter. That was possible because you were free and fearless and had a curious mind – a mind you were born with. You had no worries or anxiety and enjoyed the best health and happiness. Now you are deprived of your scientific mind, which sought reason and explanation. To enjoy the fun of life, you need to salvage your lost scientific mind. I wrote the next chapter titled The Scientific Mind in hopes that it will help you retrieve your fun moments.

The tonic of life is fun and playfulness. You see, my child, daily fun is like a daily dose of life's energy. It brings laughter and keeps us moving forward. Those who don't find joy in each day might need to rethink things. Something might be amiss in their lives. This wisdom comes from George Matthew Adams, as Ashoke Agarwal mentions in his article "Why Fun is Must in Life."

Go down the memory lane of your childhood until you spend it in a boarding house and college hostels away from home, unbounded and free from any constraint. You will distinctly recall those days full of fun and playful ventures. Your minds constantly seek fun-filled moments, wanting nothing but to amuse yourself. This playfulness is essential to nature to all beings and is the tonic of life.

You know, David Graeber had a conversation with June Thunderstorm, and she told him, "All animals play, even ants." She was a professional gardener and had seen many instances of this in nature. Graeber goes on to mention that even evolutionary psychologists have noticed playfulness everywhere in nature, even in electrons. They wonder why fun is fun and question whether electrons "choose" their actions. It's a tough question to prove, but it makes sense to consider that some form of intentionality, experience, and freedom exists at every level of physical reality, as

part of a materialist view of the world. That's the essence of what Graeber discusses in his article titled "What's the Point If We Can't Have Fun."

Electrons move as if their actions respond to stimuli as if they are conscious of what is happening around them, just as humans or any other species are conscious and respond to touching something hot. or react according to their experience. Their actions are automatic. Not only the electrons but every part of the cosmos is conscious, and their activities are taken independently and based on their experiences and the moment's need. The purpose of all the parts of the universe is to save themselves and the universe from disintegrating. "The universe is full of interconnected parts. In our Solar System, countless large objects orbit the galactic centre for hundreds of millions of years, all discussed in Ethan Siegel's article "Why Do All The Planets Orbit In The Same Plane?"

In your free days of schooling, you were self-governed; there were no outward constraints; you yourself were responsible for your life and were free to think and act as you intended/desired in your experiences, fearlessly. When you had no social conditioning and no one controlled you,   There was no fear of failure. Then you were orbiting/behaving in the same plane the planets and electrons orbit or behave. Your behaviour was natural. As natural as the other parts of the universe are natural because your mind is free, and a free mind pursues fun. The fun comes when you intend to act without any constraints, take actions as you desire and are responsible for the consequences. Whether negative or positive, the consequences of your actions leave you with invaluable experiences, and you develop and evolve fast.

In contrast, everything changes when you come in contact with social life. You acquire knowledge from society and accept it as a reality without finding its truthfulness; gradually, your mind is conditioned with this worldly knowledge.   You had not the

faintest idea how the conditioning happened, and this conditioned mind becomes your reality, an unreal reality and the cause of all troubles and chaos in life and the world.   It is a matter of great anguish that almost the whole world is a victim of social conditioning – a society whose mind is conditioned is not free to do things his way and misses the peace it wants. There cannot be peace and harmony in the world unless people are liberated from social conditions and conditionings. The only way to free oneself from the condition is to deny the things one sees. You deny it means doubting everything. When you doubt things, you want to know the reality the way you always doubted in your academic life and discuss or do an in-depth investigation to find the truth. The real fun of life is in doubting everything and exploring things thoroughly.

Before entering real life, you had the freedom to intend and think the way you desired based on your experiences and take action, which amused you, and you had fun in its entirety. Then you are naturally attentive to your heart which is perfectly aligned with cosmic consciousness. You were aligned with your heart's consciousness because you could have fun and act in whatever you thought fit. You had no doubts. Your heart never allowed you to be controlled by others and to accept instruction against your free will.

Playfulness is embedded in you and every part of the universe. What's the point if we can't have fun? Look around; you can find everylife enjoying playing. You will find even water, air, and light at play if you have a keen eye. You see, that's just how Mother Nature works. She flourishes when her children are playful and joyful. Wise mothers understand that joy comes from within and doesn't depend on external circumstances. Our ego and intellect have often led us away from this beautiful instinct in our search for logic. Thanks to our ego, we no longer pay attention to that very significant aspect of our inborn funny bones.

Let's see the fun-filled behaviours we observe in us and around us in nature. When you have the freedom, you intend to get fun out of your actions. Most often, you haven't gotten the desired result. That's why you often fail. But you undoubtedly gained experience from your failures, and you enjoyed your experience. Your experience was gratifying because you enjoyed the play of mind. Whether mental or physical, playing or actions are always gratifying, and gainful experiences are fun.

Altruism can be quite puzzling. David Graeber raises some interesting questions about it. Why would animals ever sacrifice their own well-being for others? Yet, they sometimes do. Take honeybees, for instance. When their hive is under attack, they form these intense defensive groups called 'hot defensive bee balls.' These bees literally risk their lives to protect the hive. It's a bit of a mystery because, if we try to explain it scientifically, we wonder what these kamikaze bees are trying to maximise. Their actions are quite extraordinary, and it's a fascinating topic, as Graeber points out.

Altruism is also an act without motivation, just as fun has no motives. You can observe lambs at play, birds hanging upside down, fish chasing each other for fun, and monkeys moving by hanging underneath branches and using their arms to swing between each support. They all are playing just for fun without any motivation. So are humans. If you ask children why they are playing, the answer would be "just for fun". Our ego's unrealistic craving for more and evermore disengaged us from enjoying the fun of life. Your instinct for play and fun never dies, and you often have family and friends get-togethers for fun. Though not with that freedom kids have or you had during your educational journey.

You know, child, life teaches us a valuable lesson: every second spent in unhappiness is second wasted, never to be reclaimed. People today often chase happiness through various means like

weight loss, new clothes, or seeking popularity on social media. But they sometimes forget the most important part of being happy – having fun along the way.

It might be a pleasant surprise for most to know that fun and laughter heal. Laughter is one of the most potent medicines. It brings people together and brings positive changes to your body and emotions. It boosts your immune system, lifts your mood, eases pain, and shields you from stress's harmful effects. Nothing works as swiftly and consistently as a good laugh to restore balance to your mind and body. Humour has a way of lightening your load, sparking hope, fostering connections, and keeping you centred, attentive, and lively. It even helps you let go of anger and forgive more easily.

You see, our bodies produce natural chemicals called endorphins to help us deal with pain and stress. They're often called "feel-good" chemicals because they relieve pain and boost happiness. Doctors sometimes prescribe opioid drugs to patients in pain because they trigger the release of these endorphins. It's like a quick path to pain relief and a sense of well-being. But here's the catch: when the effect wears off, some folks may want that good feeling back, and that's when the road to potential addiction can begin. However, there are cases where people find pain relief without opioids. Norman Cousins' book, "An Anatomy of Illness As Perceived by Patient," is a fine example of this.

Let me tell you about Norman Cousins, a political journalist and activist. In the 1970s, he received a bleak diagnosis: ankylosing spondylitis. The doctors said he had a one in five hundred chance of recovery, and he was looking at a life of severe physical disability. But Cousins wasn't one to give up easily. He delved into brain chemistry and believed that laughter therapy could help him. Following his doctor's advice, he took high doses of Vitamin C, maintained a healthy diet, and watched funny movies every day. It might sound astonishing, but he began to get better. In the end,

Cousins made a full recovery from his illness. He was so inspired by his experience that he wrote a memoir called "Anatomy of an Illness" to encourage other patients to take an active role in their treatment. Today, his story is celebrated as a case study of the healing power of joy and laughter therapy.

You know,   laughter is more than just a burst of joy. It's like adding rich patterns to the tapestry of our daily lives. When we laugh in response to funny moments, it's not as simple as it seems. It actually involves quite a bit of brain power because it activates various parts of the brain that handle movement, emotions, thinking, and social interactions. So, those giggles and guffaws are doing more for us than we might think!

Your academic life was vastly different from present-day situations. In school and college, you had the freedom to think and do as you desired, and the desire was to do something unique to help you distinguish yourself from others. Constantly round the clock, your mind is busy thinking to make your days full of fun and laughter. That was possible because you were free and fearless and had a curious mind – a mind you were born with. You had no worries or anxiety and enjoyed the best health and happiness. Now you are deprived of your scientific mind, which sought reason and explanation. To enjoy the fun of life, you need to salvage your lost scientific mind. I wrote the next chapter titled The Scientific Mind in hopes that it will help you retrieve your fun moments.

The tonic of life is fun and playfulness. You see, my child, daily fun is like a daily dose of life's energy. It brings laughter and keeps us moving forward. Those who don't find joy in each day might need to rethink things. Something might be amiss in their lives. This wisdom comes from George Matthew Adams, as Ashoke Agarwal mentions in his article "Why Fun is Must in Life."

Go down the memory lane of your childhood until you spend it in a boarding house and college hostels away from home, unbounded and free from any constraint. You will distinctly recall those days full of fun and playful ventures. Your minds constantly seek fun-filled moments, wanting nothing but to amuse yourself. This playfulness is essential to nature to all beings and is the tonic of life.

You know, David Graeber had a conversation with June Thunderstorm, and she told him, "All animals play, even ants." She was a professional gardener and had seen many instances of this in nature. Graeber goes on to mention that even evolutionary psychologists have noticed playfulness everywhere in nature, even in electrons. They wonder why fun is fun and question whether electrons "choose" their actions. It's a tough question to prove, but it makes sense to consider that some form of intentionality, experience, and freedom exists at every level of physical reality, as part of a materialist view of the world. That's the essence of what Graeber discusses in his article titled "What's the Point If We Can't Have Fun."

Electrons move as if their actions respond to stimuli as if they are conscious of what is happening around them, just as humans or any other species are conscious and respond to touching something hot. or react according to their experience. Their actions are automatic. Not only the electrons but every part of the cosmos is conscious, and their activities are taken independently and based on their experiences and the moment's need. The purpose of all the parts of the universe is to save themselves and the universe from disintegrating. "The universe is full of interconnected parts. In our Solar System, countless large objects orbit the galactic centre for hundreds of millions of years, all discussed in Ethan Siegel's article "Why Do All The Planets Orbit In The Same Plane?"

In your free days of schooling, you were self-governed; there were no outward constraints; you yourself were responsible for your life and were free to think and act as you intended/desired in your experiences, fearlessly. When you had no social conditioning and no one controlled you,   There was no fear of failure. Then you were orbiting/behaving in the same plane the planets and electrons orbit or behave. Your behaviour was natural. As natural as the other parts of the universe are natural because your mind is free, and a free mind pursues fun. The fun comes when you intend to act without any constraints, take actions as you desire and are responsible for the consequences. Whether negative or positive, the consequences of your actions leave you with invaluable experiences, and you develop and evolve fast.

In contrast, everything changes when you come in contact with social life. You acquire knowledge from society and accept it as a reality without finding its truthfulness; gradually, your mind is conditioned with this worldly knowledge.   You had not the faintest idea how the conditioning happened, and this conditioned mind becomes your reality, an unreal reality and the cause of all troubles and chaos in life and the world.   It is a matter of great anguish that almost the whole world is a victim of social conditioning – a society whose mind is conditioned is not free to do things his way and misses the peace it wants. There cannot be peace and harmony in the world unless people are liberated from social conditions and conditionings. The only way to free oneself from the condition is to deny the things one sees. You deny it means doubting everything. When you doubt things, you want to know the reality the way you always doubted in your academic life and discuss or do an in-depth investigation to find the truth. The real fun of life is in doubting everything and exploring things thoroughly.

Before entering real life, you had the freedom to intend and think the way you desired based on your experiences and take

action, which amused you, and you had fun in its entirety. Then you are naturally attentive to your heart which is perfectly aligned with cosmic consciousness. You were aligned with your heart's consciousness because you could have fun and act in whatever you thought fit. You had no doubts. Your heart never allowed you to be controlled by others and to accept instruction against your free will.

Playfulness is embedded in you and every part of the universe. What's the point if we can't have fun? Look around; you can find everylife enjoying playing. You will find even water, air, and light at play if you have a keen eye. You see, that's just how Mother Nature works. She flourishes when her children are playful and joyful. Wise mothers understand that joy comes from within and doesn't depend on external circumstances. Our ego and intellect have often led us away from this beautiful instinct in our search for logic. Thanks to our ego, we no longer pay attention to that very significant aspect of our inborn funny bones.

Let's see the fun-filled behaviours we observe in us and around us in nature. When you have the freedom, you intend to get fun out of your actions. Most often, you haven't gotten the desired result. That's why you often fail. But you undoubtedly gained experience from your failures, and you enjoyed your experience. Your experience was gratifying because you enjoyed the play of mind. Whether mental or physical, playing or actions are always gratifying, and gainful experiences are fun.

Altruism can be quite puzzling. David Graeber raises some interesting questions about it. Why would animals ever sacrifice their own well-being for others? Yet, they sometimes do. Take honeybees, for instance. When their hive is under attack, they form these intense defensive groups called 'hot defensive bee balls.' These bees literally risk their lives to protect the hive. It's a bit of a mystery because, if we try to explain it scientifically, we wonder what these kamikaze bees are trying to maximise. Their actions are quite extraordinary, and it's a fascinating topic, as Graeber points

out.

Altruism is also an act without motivation, just as fun has no motives. You can observe lambs at play, birds hanging upside down, fish chasing each other for fun, and monkeys moving by hanging underneath branches and using their arms to swing between each support. They all are playing just for fun without any motivation. So are humans. If you ask children why they are playing, the answer would be "just for fun". Our ego's unrealistic craving for more and evermore disengaged us from enjoying the fun of life. Your instinct for play and fun never dies, and you often have family and friends get-togethers for fun. Though not with that freedom kids have or you had during your educational journey.

You know, child, life teaches us a valuable lesson: every second spent in unhappiness is second wasted, never to be reclaimed. People today often chase happiness through various means like weight loss, new clothes, or seeking popularity on social media. But they sometimes forget the most important part of being happy – having fun along the way.

It might be a pleasant surprise for most to know that fun and laughter heal. Laughter is one of the most potent medicines. It brings people together and brings positive changes to your body and emotions. It boosts your immune system, lifts your mood, eases pain, and shields you from stress's harmful effects. Nothing works as swiftly and consistently as a good laugh to restore balance to your mind and body. Humour has a way of lightening your load, sparking hope, fostering connections, and keeping you centred, attentive, and lively. It even helps you let go of anger and forgive more easily.

You see, our bodies produce natural chemicals called endorphins to help us deal with pain and stress. They're often called "feel-good" chemicals because they relieve pain and boost happiness. Doctors sometimes prescribe opioid drugs to patients

in pain because they trigger the release of these endorphins. It's like a quick path to pain relief and a sense of well-being. But here's the catch: when the effect wears off, some folks may want that good feeling back, and that's when the road to potential addiction can begin. However, there are cases where people find pain relief without opioids. Norman Cousins' book, "An Anatomy of Illness As Perceived by Patient," is a fine example of this.

Let me tell you about Norman Cousins, a political journalist and activist. In the 1970s, he received a bleak diagnosis: ankylosing spondylitis. The doctors said he had a one in five hundred chance of recovery, and he was looking at a life of severe physical disability. But Cousins wasn't one to give up easily. He delved into brain chemistry and believed that laughter therapy could help him. Following his doctor's advice, he took high doses of Vitamin C, maintained a healthy diet, and watched funny movies every day. It might sound astonishing, but he began to get better. In the end, Cousins made a full recovery from his illness. He was so inspired by his experience that he wrote a memoir called "Anatomy of an Illness" to encourage other patients to take an active role in their treatment. Today, his story is celebrated as a case study of the healing power of joy and laughter therapy.

You know,   laughter is more than just a burst of joy. It's like adding rich patterns to the tapestry of our daily lives. When we laugh in response to funny moments, it's not as simple as it seems. It actually involves quite a bit of brain power because it activates various parts of the brain that handle movement, emotions, thinking, and social interactions. So, those giggles and guffaws are doing more for us than we might think!

Your academic life was vastly different from present-day situations. In school and college, you had the freedom to think and do as you desired, and the desire was to do something unique to help you distinguish yourself from others. Constantly round the

clock, your mind is busy thinking to make your days full of fun and laughter. That was possible because you were free and fearless and had a curious mind – a mind you were born with. You had no worries or anxiety and enjoyed the best health and happiness. Now you are deprived of your scientific mind, which sought reason and explanation. To enjoy the fun of life, you need to salvage your lost scientific mind. I wrote the next chapter titled The Scientific Mind in hopes that it will help you retrieve your fun moments.

CHAPTER FIVE

THE SCIENTIFIC MIND

"Curiosity is the mother of all knowledge," my friend, and that's a fact! I couldn't agree more with the wisdom of Roy T. Bennett when he says, "Listen with curiosity, speak with honesty, and act with integrity." Communication is about understanding, not just replying.

You know, science has shown that our brains grow faster, and we make unique connections when we follow our curiosity, especially in our early years. Life, with its ups and downs, is quite a journey. I've always been curious, trying to unravel the hidden meanings behind words. The great Albert Einstein, too, encouraged us never to stop questioning and to embrace the mystery of life every day. Curiosity truly has its own reason for being, and it's a beautiful thing to nurture.

You know, from my teenage years onward, I've had this intuitive drive to ponder the profound mysteries of eternity, life, and the wondrous structure of reality. It's as if this curiosity has been a constant companion on my life's journey, leading me to explore the deeper questions that often go unanswered. Eventually, my access to the internet was a great boon for finding answers to my quarries. René Descartes's proposition, "Cogito, ergo sum, " meaning, "I think. Therefore I am", and Deepak Chopra's "I am, therefore I think," gave me a good insight into Life. After all, our imagination and our thoughts make everything real. When a Post correspondent interviewed Albert Einstein back in 1929, his perspective on thought processes was quite fascinating. He didn't emphasise careful reasoning and calculations. Instead, he spoke of the belief in intuitions and inspirations, that inner sense of being right even when unsure. Einstein saw himself as an artist, drawing upon his imagination, and he boldly stated that imagination holds more significance than knowledge. In his view, knowledge is confined, while imagination has the power to encompass the entire world. This perspective from Einstein is a testament to the profound role that imagination plays in shaping our understanding of the universe.

My curiosity inspired me to discover a little about philosophy and spiritualism. People under the influence of culture keep a distance from people who have philosophical views. Talks about philosophy often make people uneasy and fearful. Fear is a mighty force because there is a chance of failure. Being able to take on something you thought was impossible in your own abilities was inconceivable. This thought makes you less confident. But you can make the impossible possible if you can overcome your fears. Fear wants to save you from danger. Parents and society warn children against life's risks, thus unknowingly instilling fear in them to be cautious of the threats of an uncertain future. But fear makes them timid and cowardly. They start fearing everything. It is so powerful that people dare not to know the reality of fear. It would help if you dared to see the truth of fear, especially when your upbringing didn't apprise you of its unreality. For example, when people encounter discomfort or challenging situations, they often withdraw into their thoughts or isolate themselves to avoid facing unpleasant thoughts or interactions. This tendency can ultimately make them feel even worse. What many people don't realise is that understanding the reality of a situation can help dispel fears. As Dale Carnegie wisely put it, "You can conquer almost any fear if you will only make up your mind to do so. For, remember, fear doesn't exist anywhere except in the mind." Fear, in many cases, is a major source of suffering.

To overcome fear, you need to regain your Scientific Mind, which you were born with and deprived of because of cultural pressure, the reason for our failing education system. Neither the teachers nor the parents are really involved in comprehending and developing the uniqueness of each student, and children are forced into a mode of competition culture – a culture in which children cannot apply their scientific minds. Conscious parents realised the failing system of education that gave rise to homeschooling. Homeschooling in the United States has been rapidly growing. In 2007, around 1.5 million children were homeschooled, a significant increase from 2003 and 1999, with 1.1 million and 850,000 homeschooled children, respectively. As of 2022, the number has reached approximately 3.1 million homeschoolers. Homeschooling can be an innovative approach to education, especially when parents are self-aware. Self-aware parents are effective coaches for their kids, and online teachers can also be hired to create an optimal learning environment that helps children reach their full potential.

As schools have poor learning environments, they cannot pay attention to children's unique needs; homeschooling can give them a relaxed atmosphere. At home, there is no need for competition. Instead, parents challenge them according to their ability, making education fun, and both parents and children enjoy it. There are some indirect benefits: travelling time is saved; no worry about school performance; no race for the competition; no rivalries with other students; no use of motorised vehicles to and from school hence no carbon footprint etc. My mind never changed. It remained scientific throughout my Life. Of course, it wavered at times but always returned to its authentic self. A scientific mind questions everything, seeking answers and explanations from the edges of the universe to the meaning of existence. It scrutinises facts, uncovers underlying patterns, and embraces the truth, no matter how bitter. Finding beauty in complexity and simplicity, it dissects everyday life for deeper meaning. Unaffected by others' opinions, it filters everything through its acquired knowledge. This mind dives into minutiae, making the workings of its subjects intuitive and seeks to reason out every exposure. It takes on challenges beyond its scope and revels in breaking things down to their elementary constituents, finding beauty and awe even in the smallest entities.

Children are born with natural curiosity; it is something that is ingrained in their DNA. It wants to know the truth of life from the moment they are born because of innate abilities - sensory abilities, instinct, sense of right and wrong, curiosity, intuition, etc. When the parents take cognizance of these inborn abilities, they provide a suitable atmosphere for learning. The famous lines, "the child is the father of the man," from William Shakespeare's poem "The Rainbow," highlight how childhood shapes our views. Michelle Balani, in her article "Encouraging curiosity in kids: Here is what to know," emphasises that children are born curious and thrive on exploration, questions, and imagination, leading to joyful learning. Unfortunately, this innate curiosity often fades as children grow due to parental unawareness. In Andrea K. McDaniels' piece, "Babies learn from the unexpected, Hopkins research shows," she discusses how infants possess innate knowledge and thrive when their expectations are challenged. Children are born with a clean slate, eager to explore and learn from the unknown.

"The only true wisdom is in knowing you know nothing", - said Socrates. That makes babies the wisest person. When you know nothing, your thirst for knowing everything motivates you to study and investigate. Your desire to learn more about everything means you have a scientific mind. Every baby's attitude exclaims, "I know nothing; I want to know everything," showcasing their innate curiosity and scientific sense. But what fuels this curiosity in babies? According to the article "Encouraging curiosity in preschoolers: Here is what to know," children's natural curiosity arises from their constant learning through experiences and social interactions. Preschoolers and kindergarteners, known for their active imaginations, thrive on curiosity to explore both their emotions and the world around them. Contrary to the standard belief in a "blank slate," children possess an inner voice—an innate, intuitive sense—that inspires their boundless curiosity. This voice has many names: Code of Honor and Inner Guide. Moral Code, Sense of Duty, Zameer Ki Aawaaz, Inner Voice, Personal Calling etc. Babies' inspiration comes from their callings. A baby doesn't understand the language. The only voice it takes cognizance of is its inner voice. But as they grow, its inner voice weakens in the cacophony of voices emanating from around him; though its challenges never die, they fade out. It often surfaces whenever there are conflicting opinions. But self-doubt and compulsion of cultural obligations send it into dormancy, though potentially always able to achieve expression. All my life, I was tuned with my callings. Though, my timidity often puzzled me. But with time, the voice became more assertive, wanting to know Life's mysteries. It was my intuition; I have always been tuned to it. However, I realised the reality quite late in Life. Intuition is an excellent guide, and babies are born with their inner focus. If they get the proper support, they outshine in Life.

Babies embody innocence, pure joy, and a deep connection to life. Everything they encounter is as pure as themselves, radiating joy and love unreservedly.   Parents want their babies to grow into happy and confident beings who can quickly love and inspire others. But parents and society's disposition toward a traditional lifestyle doesn't allow children to remain pure and scientific. There is scientific proof that unborn babies start learning language and music in the prenatal chamber. Conscious parents recognize the importance of establishing a secure attachment with their baby before birth. Regularly connecting with your baby in the womb, especially through music like Debussy, conveys love, welcome, and acknowledgement of their unique experience, ultimately nurturing a deep connection from the very beginning of life. Studies have shown that babies have prenatal memory and in-utero learning, emphasising the significance of early interactions, as demonstrated by De-Mause and the experiments involving Debussy's music. Unborn babies start listening to their mothers' speech during the last ten weeks of pregnancy, influencing their abilities at birth. Even six-month-old babies respond to rhythmic music with dance-like movements, showing an innate connection to music. Music has healing powers, benefiting mental health and reducing depression and anxiety. It can also help retrain the brain's right hemisphere for language functions lost due to brain damage, known as the "Kenny Rogers Effect."

Every child is special and unique. No two children have the same combination of talents. But, in a class of 40/50, the modern education system provides the same education. The system doesn't train teachers to study every child's learning style. As such, children don't get the opportunity to learn things according to their speciality. The Multigrade Teacher's Handbook of the Philippines emphasises that each child is a unique individual with distinct qualities in various aspects of life, including social, emotional, intellectual, and physical attributes. While children may share common needs and characteristics based on their age or developmental stage, it's crucial for parents and teachers to recognize and respect the individuality of each child.

Homeschooling perhaps came into existence when people realised that schools could not be emotionally warm to children, nor could they provide where children can have the freedom to exploit their unique abilities.

CHAPTER SIX

THE ZYGOTE

This chapter is all about how science and our well-being come together. It's about those tiny things inside our amazing bodies that work together to make sure we can achieve whatever we set our minds to. I am sure by now you do know how fertilisation and embryo development occur in humans.

The process of human development begins with the union of a sperm cell and an egg cell, forming a single-cell organism known as a zygote. This zygote undergoes rapid division and multiplication, progressing from a single cell to multiple cells, eventually becoming a complex human organism consisting of trillions of cells. It can be likened to the remarkable metamorphosis of a caterpillar into a butterfly, highlighting the incredible journey from a single zygote to a fully developed, organised collection of cells, tissues, and organs. From a biological point of view, a Zygote is a Human being. Dianne N. Irving, M.A., PhD, unequivocally asserts that, from a scientific standpoint, there is no doubt that a newly formed human being results from fertilisation. A human zygote is not a mere potential or possibility; it is an existing human being, albeit in its early stage, with the inherent potential for growth and development.

This huge collection of cells, tissues and organs is all multicellular organisms, whether plant or animal, including human organisms or the body. A human organism, you can say a colony inhabited by 30-40 trillion cells.   These trillions of cells make up the human body. There are 200 plus types of cells from the 80 known organisms and identify the active genes in these cells. The human body is composed of an astonishing number of cells, with an estimated average of approximately 37.2 trillion cells. These cells make up the various tissues and organs in our bodies. Additionally, the composition of the human body in terms of atoms is equally remarkable. In a typical 70 kg human, there are nearly seven octillion atoms, primarily consisting of hydrogen, oxygen, and carbon, which together account for 99% of the total. Atoms, the fundamental building blocks of matter, consist of a nucleus containing positively charged protons and neutral neutrons, surrounded by shells of negatively charged electrons, each orbiting at different energy levels.

We know that 70% of our body is water (in infants, water content is up to 78%). Water is a molecule that consists of 2 atoms of hydrogen and one of oxygen. Carbon, too, is a molecule of 12 atoms. These three add up to 99%. The rest are atoms of other molecules like potassium, sulphur, sodium, chlorine, and magnesium. There are more than 109 types of known atoms. Only 11 types make up the human body which is necessary for life. Water is present in every part of our body – cells, organs, tissues, bones, nails, hair, etc.

Without a doubt, the human organism or any organism – plant, animal or human organism - comprises these energy particles - atoms. Energies are not static – electrons are constantly vibrating. The dance of electrons around the nucleus of an atom is driven by the attraction between their negative charge and the positive charge of the nucleus. This constant movement within atoms fills what might otherwise appear as empty space. What's fascinating is that these electrons vibrate at distinct frequencies, with higher-frequency vibrations associated with positive qualities and feelings, while lower-frequency vibrations are linked to negative emotions.

This underscores the concept that the human body is essentially a dynamic interplay of energy particles, including atoms, subatomic particles, and quantum entities, all in a constant state of motion. They are always in continuous flow. They move and vibrate without stopping, even for the smallest part of the time. An atom is made of protons, neutrons, and electrons. Protons and neutrons are in the nucleus, around which electrons move at an incredible speed of 2200 km a second. At that speed, one can make a round trip to the Earth in 18 seconds.

These clarifications were required to bring home the hard truth that the human body is a colony of 30/40 trillion cells; each cell consists of 100 trillion energy particles - atoms. Cells, like a zygote, are conscious human beings. Cells are compassionately dedicated to the well-being of the whole colony called the human body. In the colony of the body, the cells cohabit in perfect harmony. Even if there is a small paper cut in any body part, all body cells get obsessed with stopping the bleeding. Under a powerful microscope, you can observe the zeal and altruism with which each cell of the body is charged to sacrifice itself to stop the bleeding and heal the cut to save the colony, just like mothers who are always ready to self-sacrifice for their loved ones. "The simplest approach to monitoring cell migration is the so-called "scratch" assay. A pipette tip or other sharp object is used to gouge a scratch or "wound" in a confluent cell monolayer. Then a microscope is used to observe cells filling in or "repairing" the wound."- article Measuring Cell Migration.   "As soon as the paper cuts into the cells of your skin, your body springs into action. First, blood cells called platelets join together at the paper cut and form a clot to stop the bleeding. The platelets then release chemicals called cytokines into your bloodstream. Cytokines attract attention. When your skin is cut, your body initiates a series of responses to heal the wound. Initially, platelets in your blood come together to form a clot, stopping the bleeding. These platelets release cytokines, which are chemical messengers. Cytokines play a crucial role in attracting specific cells to the injury site to initiate the healing process and activate your immune system. This healing mechanism is essential for repairing damaged tissues and restoring your skin's integrity.

Cells, even the simplest prokaryotic ones, are believed to possess a form of consciousness and sentience. This consciousness allows them to respond to various signals and external stimuli. Cells have receptors that bind to signalling molecules, triggering physiological responses. In the context of the immune system, this cellular consciousness plays a crucial role in defending the body against infections and diseases by keeping cells vigilant and ready to fight off invading pathogens.

....

Maintaining good health is essential, and your immune system plays a vital role in keeping you well. Pathogens, such as viruses, bacteria, parasites, and fungi, can make you sick – to stay healthy, it's crucial to understand that your immune system is your body's defence against these invaders. According to the "Health Encyclopedia," your immune system comprises special cells, tissues, and organs that work together to protect you. Taking care of your cells' health is key to supporting your overall well-being. When your immune system is strong, it can fend off various disease-causing germs and even cancer cells, as mentioned in the article "How the Immune System Protects You From Infection." So, remember to lead a lifestyle that promotes cell health and strengthens your immune system, helping you stay resilient against illnesses.

Immunological memory is the immune system's ability to swiftly recognize previously encountered antigens and trigger corresponding immune responses, typically observed in secondary and subsequent reactions. Dorothy M. Neddermyer, PhD, explains that universal Laws assert the interconnectedness of all things, rooted in the belief that the universe consists of energy, including us, and this energy circulates. At the microscopic level, we are a dynamic collection of rapidly spinning electrons and energy atoms, intimately connected to this vast sea of whirling energy. She adds that our beliefs, thoughts, emotions, words, and actions all embody energy. They shape our realities as energy operates in cycles. The collective beliefs, thoughts, feelings, words, and actions of everyone on Earth shape our shared consciousness and the world we perceive.

My dears, the human body is no different, as it is a part of the universe and a powerful energy system. Whether we recognize it or not, our existence is fundamentally composed of vibrating energy. Humans are formed from cells, which, in turn, are made up of atoms that essentially vibrate with energy. This energy operates at various frequencies, and our emotions are linked to these frequencies. When our frequency exceeds 500 on a scale of 0 to 1000, we feel joyful and at peace. However, challenges arise when the frequency falls below 500, leading to emotions like shame at 20. Emotions vary along this scale from guilt, apathy, and grief to desire, anger, pride, courage, neutrality, willingness, acceptance, and reason. Love prevails at 500, followed by joy, and as we ascend further, we experience peace, enlightenment, and an elevated state of being, as discussed in Christie Marrie Sheldon's video titled "Change Your Frequency, Change Your Reality."

That makes it pretty evident that the secret to total wellness lies in managing the frequency of your body's energy. As you are the owner of your body, only you can manage the frequency of your body. Only you have the power to accomplish this task. When you can keep your energy level high, you enjoy good health. Only you can create that healthy environment by ensuring that the oscillating energy frequency mostly remains above or around 500. Good health ensures that your immune system and all other bodily functions operate optimally. It's a fact that when your body, including the immune system, is shielded from environmental threats and supported by healthy lifestyle choices, it functions more effectively. This underscores the importance of regulating your body's energy frequency by refining your way of life. This leads to the essential question: how can you effectively manage your body's energy?

Start questioning even the correctness of your habits. All questions must be related to your health and wellness; everything exists when you exist; you exist for as long as you are living. But only living is not enough. We must know how to achieve total health - physical, mental, emotional and spiritual. If you are unwell, you are confused and sick. If you are sick, you cannot reason sensibly. When fully aware, you start seeing the gut-brain connection. Seeing the gut-brain connection helps you choose the right food and habit that keeps you in perfect health. Certain food groups can have a positive impact on the gut-brain axis and potentially enhance brain health by altering the gut bacteria composition, as explained by Ruairi Robertson, PhD in Healthline's article "The Gut-Brain Connection: How it Works and The Role of Nutrition."

The gut-brain connection is a complex system involving around 500 million neurons in the gut that send information to and from the brain. Additionally, the vagus nerve acts as a bridge between the gut and the brain, transmitting sensory information and signals. Furthermore, the gut houses a microbiome consisting of various microorganisms that aid in digestion and produce neurotransmitters, which can influence neuronal activity. This intricate network can lead to experiences like nervousness causing nausea or excitement leading to "butterflies in your stomach." Conversely, the gut can send signals to the brain, emphasising the importance of dietary choices, including the incorporation of more prebiotics and probiotics.

Water has been proven to be consciousness and has a memory. I will spend more time detailing this in the next chapter. Our body is 70% water. As such, every part of the human body, every cell of the body, is conscious and has memory. The memory within our immune system retains information and reacts accordingly to combat invading pathogens, protecting us from illnesses. When a pathogen attacks, the immune system's response involves the production of pathogen-specific antigens directed by cytokines, as explained in the article "What are Cytokines." This process allows the immune system to swiftly identify and eliminate the pathogen.

Furthermore, the immune system plays a vital role in the self-regulation, self-repair, and self-healing of the human body. Hormones and neuropeptides, such as oxytocin, dopamine, serotonin, and opiates, are immunomodulators that enhance these self-healing and self-repair mechanisms, as noted by Deepak Chopra

The human body is the most sophisticated and complex machine.   It is a great machine that regulates, repairs and heals itself. Like other machines, human machines also need suitable energy to work at their best. Just as any machine needs unique pure energy - petrol-driven automobiles cannot run on diesel – the human body, too, needs pure fuel suitable to it. Similar to how an automobile relies solely on gasoline as its fuel source, the human body operates using a single type of energy: chemical energy. To be more precise, the body exclusively utilises a particular form of chemical energy for its biological processes, known as adenosine triphosphate (ATP). This molecule serves as the primary source of energy for various cellular activities, as explained in the article titled "How the Body Uses Energy." Unhealthy living practices like lack of exercise or consuming unhealthy dead foods weaken our immune system and cells get sick; our bodies suffer. The best pure fuel for humans is live food found nowhere else except in the lap of Mother Nature: fresh fruits, vegetables, herbs, whole grains, pulses, dry fruits, pure water, pure air, and pure solar energy. Anything that comes directly from nature unprocessed is best for the human machine. Factory-processed packaged foods are highly harmful to human consumption. They are the slow poison that damages our immune system, and we get sick, and often deadly diseases strike. I'm sure you know this: weak immunity attracts infectious diseases and viruses the most. But getting pure energy for the body is not an easy task. You have to educate yourself and follow a strict 24-hour regime for your total wellness. What you should do immediately is stop consuming dead, processed food and switch over to live foods. If possible, consume organic fresh live food. That will resolve most of your nutritional problems, and many health issues will be self-resolved or self-healed. With the increase in take-out and home delivery of meals, you should also know that you can keep diseases at bay by keeping your gut bacteria healthy. Consuming live foods and probiotics is the best way to keep them healthy.

Another thing you should know is that the cause of diseases could be circadian rhythm disorder. These disruptions in your sleep patterns can either be temporary and linked to factors like your sleep habits, occupation, or travel, or they can be persistent and result from factors such as ageing, genetics, or underlying medical conditions. This insight is outlined in the article titled "What Are Circadian Rhythm Disorders?"

Without perfect disease-free health, you live in fear of uncertainty. Fear of uncertainty often stems from a fear of losing control. When we believe we can't influence future outcomes, we start to anticipate disaster, leading to significant anxiety, especially for those who struggle with uncertainty. Anxiety can manifest as concerns about serious illness, and the stress it brings can mimic the physical symptoms of sickness. These sensations, like stomach discomfort and nausea, can be attributed to anxiety rather than an actual illness, as highlighted in information from "Calm Clinic."

To effectively manage health anxiety, it's crucial to cultivate self-awareness. Recognizing your thoughts and emotions enables you to control them better. I strongly believe that lacking self-awareness can lead to negative emotions and difficulty aligning your choices with your desires.

You know, the human mind has limitless potential. Think about it, our brains have about 100 billion nerve cells, and each of them connects with about 10,000 others. These connections can switch on or off in countless ways. When you consider all the different ways each human mind can connect with others on this planet, it's like an infinite universe of possibilities, as Susan Rosenthal explains in her article on 'The Infinite Potential of the Human Mind.'

Every human is endowed with this infinite power concealed in him from his very birth. Given the proper guidance, anyone can turn his desires into reality. People think babies are born with a clean slate, and parents and societies try their best to write a program in their minds to help the child achieve the best in his life. Their intentions are not evil; only their knowledge is limited. According to the prevailing culture, once a person's mind is programmed early in childhood, it becomes almost impossible to change it unless they are put under able guidance. Unfortunately, people are unwilling to listen to reason. Their beliefs are so powerful as if they are put under the spell of some unknown spirit.

Anxiety has deep roots in our minds and bodies. Don't hesitate to seek help, whether it's from me or those you trust the most. If you uncover the reasons behind your anxiety and deal with them wisely, I believe you can lessen its impact on your nerves. Eating well, staying active, doing what makes you happy, practising mindfulness, and reflecting on life regularly – these are the keys to embracing the frequency of life.

CHAPTER SEVEN

THE PUZZLES OF LIFE

The desire to raise mentally strong and healthy children and the passion for passing on life lessons to them remains inherent in all parents. At least, it is true for me, although communicating every experience to children is not possible. I am very conscious of my helplessness on this matter. Still, whenever I learn something vital, I become restless. The burden of not passing on my responsibility lingers. Though my responsibility can never end, I am writing this book to cut back on my responsibilities. I feel a sense of achievement before achieving anything as I write this book. When you are trying anything for a cause, you have a sense of accomplishment in every moment of life - you feel joy in every moment. The source of this passion is nothing but love, limitless love for you and humanity. A love that allows me to celebrate every moment of life. And this is what matters. Nothing can be more gratifying than a genuine loving concern.

Once Albert Einstein said, "I have no special talent. I am only passionately curious." You need to be passionately curious to know life's puzzles. Life always puzzled me because I was always curious to know life's secret. I wanted to know how everything evolved and how life came into existence. I don't know how much of it you know, but I wish to tell you what I know. Indeed, the universe began with the Big Bang, and stars have been creating heavier elements like carbon, oxygen, and neon through supernova explosions. In an article on One Mind - One Energy, it's explained that everything in the universe is made of energy, which is the basic building block of matter. This energy is in a constant state of flux, following the Universal Law of Perpetual Transmutation of Energy. It's the same energy that composes our bodies, our homes, cars, phones, and everything else. This universal energy can neither be created nor destroyed, and it underlies all forms and shapes in the universe, originating from a realm of pure energy.

Astrophysicists suggest that all the matter in the universe, including everything on Earth, stars, and galaxies, was formed at the universe's inception roughly 13 billion years ago, as noted by CERN. This matter, which includes our bodies, is essentially "condensed energy." This concept reinforces the idea that "Everything is energy, everything is one, and everything is possible." Effective energy management becomes key to realising this potential because, fundamentally, everything is energy.

The above explanation leaves no doubt that the source of everything is energy. Albert Einstein's famous equation, $E=MC2$, confirms this theory. The equation means "Energy equals mass times the speed of light squared." On the most basic level, the equation says that energy and mass (matter) are interchangeable; they are different forms of the same thing. Under the right conditions, energy can become mass and vice versa. Yet, in other words, you can say everything in the universe, whether visible or invisible, including the five elements - water, air, fire, earth, and space - are different kinds of energy. Even our thoughts, emotions, consciousness, and imaginations are energy. And all matters that are visible to our eyes in the world or space are nothing but "condensed energy." B. Hicks says, "All matter is merely energy condensed to a slow vibration."

In the article "Everything is Energy, Everything is One, Everything is Possible" by Hans Anderegg, it's emphasised that everything in the universe, including the oceans, the sky, living beings, and our thoughts and feelings, are interconnected through energy. All these elements originate from a common source and are interrelated, highlighting the idea that everything is one. The energy of our thoughts and emotions influences both the world and everyone in it, empowering us to shape our own reality as our minds govern over matter.

Mind rules over matter. The mind always ruled over matter. The mind can manage matters, energy and consciousness. All the advances in technology are the creation of the mind. Science advanced significantly as scientists harnessed the ability to manipulate energy particles, including atoms, subatomic, and quantum particles. They achieved this by quantizing classical field theory, and restricting fields to discrete units called "quanta." Beyond photons (the quanta of light), scientists like Paul Dirac extended this concept to encompass electrons and all other particles. According to quantum field theory, particles are manifestations of quantum fields that permeate all of space, as explained in the article "What is Particle" in Quanta magazine.

Johnny Wood's article "Consciousness is A Big Problem For Science" discusses materialist science's attempt to explain consciousness as a product of complex brain processes, suggesting that the mind is solely a result of neurons firing in the brain. However, there is no concrete neurological evidence to substantiate this theory, and some researchers argue that these scientists may be looking in the wrong direction or employing inadequate methods. Deepak Chopra describes consciousness as something beyond our senses but essential for perception. It's intangible yet vital for our ability to touch and feel. He emphasises that our world is trying to awaken to this profound concept called "consciousness." This, he does in an article titled "Consciousness and Discontinuity Remarks by Deepak Chopra at Be The Change" on World Business Academy,

When asked about panpsychism by Gareth Cook, philosopher Phillips Goff simplifies it: Panpsychism suggests that consciousness exists everywhere in the universe as a fundamental aspect. This doesn't imply everything is conscious, but rather that even the tiniest components of reality, like electrons and quarks, possess basic forms of experience. The intricate experiences of the human or animal brain are believed to emerge from the experiences of these fundamental components.

Understanding consciousness in everything may seem complex, but one clear example is water. According to an article on 'The Wellness Enterprise' titled "Dr. Masaru Emoto And Water Consciousness," Dr. Masaru Emoto, a Japanese scientist, explored how thoughts and vibrations impact the molecular structure of water. His research, involving high-speed photography of water crystals, revealed that the most beautiful crystals formed when water was exposed to the words "love and gratitude." Water crystals don't just form from love and gratitude; they change when exposed to human words, thoughts, sounds, and intentions. In his book 'The Hidden Messages in Water,' Dr. Emoto shows that loving and compassionate intentions create pleasing water structures, while fearful intentions create disfigured ones. He used Magnetic Resonance Analysis and high-speed photos for this. Dr. Emoto also explored how sound affects water. Classical music, for example, generates beautiful patterns, while heavy metal music creates distorted ones. Water molecules, consisting of atoms and subatomic particles like electrons, neutrons, and protons, make up around 70% of our body weight. This implies the potential for consciousness in atoms and subatomic energy particles.

Since everything in the universe is a form of energy, the idea of consciousness being everywhere is compelling. As mentioned earlier, our body comprises around 70% water, with each of our 30-40 trillion cells containing water. This suggests that our cells have some form of consciousness, and our activities, influenced by our senses, impact our health. The article on Omar Itani's website emphasises that our thoughts shape our reality, quoting philosophers and thinkers who stress the importance of our thoughts in defining our lives.

Dr. Emoto's work shows water's consciousness. Atoms, the building blocks of matter, are not solid but composed of subatomic particles, as Deepak Chopra explains in "Boundless Energy." This suggests that condensed energy, like water, could have consciousness. Everything with water, from oceans to the human body, may have some form of consciousness, given that the entire universe is energy-based. Chopra's book also highlights that atoms within the human body are mostly empty spaces, similar to intergalactic voids.

The article "How Thoughts Create the World and Reality" on Speaking Tree underscores how thoughts can shape one's reality and destiny. It emphasises controlling thoughts and imagination to attract desired experiences and highlights that circumstances in life stem from inner thoughts and beliefs. I too, have since an early age worked profusely on understanding and reshaping my thoughts. I know for a fact that it has immensely influenced my life.

In an interview with Omega, Deepak Chopra discusses the perspective that the universe, body, and mind exist within consciousness as perceptual experiences. He suggests that there's only consciousness and that it's gaining acceptance in scientific circles, even among physicists and neuroscientists. This view posits consciousness as fundamental, with everything else, including the mind and matter, as secondary, as described in his article "The Last Paradox: Does the Universe Have a Mind?"

As earlier said, subatomic particles are not solid, tangible objects; they also are fluctuations of energy that have taken on a material form. Einstein proposed that matter is essentially energy in a different form, a concept affirmed by physicists in the 1920s and 1930s who described physical particles as energy vibrations known as "wave functions." This revelation, known as "wave-particle duality" in quantum physics, signifies that matter is fundamentally composed of wave vibrations. Deepak Chopra further explores this notion, suggesting that our bodies go beyond their material appearance. They are dynamic fields of energy, with individual particles being energy vibrations within a larger universal field. This underlying "quantum mechanical body" consists of pure energy and intelligence, shaping the material body. Understanding this quantum body may hold the key to addressing chronic fatigue and other health issues.

Deepak Chopra discusses a new field called mind/body medicine, emphasising that viewing the body as solid and the mind as insubstantial hinders understanding their interaction. Recognizing that the body is pure energy highlights the similarity between thought and matter. According to quantum physics, thoughts are subtle vibrations within the unified field, influencing bodily functions significantly.

Anyways, the subject is extremely complex and beyond the perceptions of ordinary people like us. However, one thing must be kept in mind: "The universe is governed by many different universal laws such as the Law of Attraction, Law of Vibration, Law of Cause and Effect, and the Law of Forgiveness. Law of Abundance, Law of Polarity, Law of Perpetual Transmutation, Law of Rhythm, the Law of Sacrifice, and many more," as the website "One Mind - One Energy" explains. And the most consequential of them all is the "Universal Law of Love".

When this universe was made, a system was set up. Those who had NDE were shown the core principle of the universe: the law of love. If we harm others, we'll feel pain. If we love others, we'll feel love. This law is so simple, that even a child can grasp it. No need for a fancy degree or years of research. In the East, it's known as the law of karma, akin to a law of physics: "For every action, there is a reaction."   The Bible calls it, "As you sow, so shall you reap."
In her HuffPost post titled "Law of Love and Compassion," Thierry Dufay validates the idea that the law of love is the most significant for our lives, bringing happiness to individuals and all of humanity. Leo Tolstoy originally wrote these words, which eventually reached Mohandas Karamchand Gandhi. Love has the power to transform enemies into friends, as Gandhi stated, and human compassion connects us not out of pity but as beings who turn suffering into hope.

Baruch Spinoza, a philosopher, noted that those governed by reason seek what is useful to themselves following reason and desire the same for all of humanity, making them just, faithful, and honourable in their conduct.

Through consciousness, we can gauge our energy levels. When we cultivate love, compassion, forgiveness, and empathy, we fulfil a higher purpose, benefiting not just others but also ourselves and, in the process, the entire universe.

CHAPTER EIGHT

PUZZLE OF THE UNIVERSE

The Big Bang Theory, explained by Elizabeth Howell in "Space," tells us the universe started small and expanded over 13.8 billion years, forming atoms like helium and hydrogen along the way. Stars emerged about 100 million years after the Big Bang, and galaxies took nearly a billion years to spread across the cosmos, as Scientific American notes. Life began with single-celled organisms 3.5 billion years ago, evolving into more complex forms around 600 million years ago, per NASA.

Around 1.8 million years ago, human intelligence and brain size grew significantly, as discussed in Smithsonian Magazine's "How Smart Were Early Humans?" This brain expansion led to cognitive and mental skill development.

Lastly, humans, the last species in evolution, possess the highest complexity, according to Borje Ekstig's article, "Complexity, Natural Selection, and the Evolution of Life and Humans."

Humans are the most intelligent animals on Earth – this, of course, is by human standards. And its thinking capacity made its life mysterious. It has been a mystery since humans got the gift of intelligence and the power of imagination. I believe that people fear mystery. Fear makes the mystery even more mysterious. Though metaphysical science and philosophy have unravelled many secrets, it is hard for people to understand them. Even the educated fear, and abstain from venturing into the unknown. They do not wish to know the reality simply because of the thousands of years of dogmatic teaching that has conditioned their mind. The beliefs are so firmly embedded in their psyche that even a thought of thinking against it would seem to be rebelling against the gods. Rebelling against the almighty obviously, fills them with fear. But one has to be rebellious to unravel the mysteries of the universe, mysteries of life and death.

Before revealing the mysteries of life, you should know that many people who know the mysteries of life and the universe do not fear anything. Such people don't fear anything. Isn't it incredible to know that there are people who live free from any fears? I am an example. I, too, do not fear anything. If I fear anything, it is the fear of annoying you, my people, or any soul on earth. I fear not because I know the reality; I don't let my emotions rule me; I have learned how to manage my emotions. Not that I always had been fearless. My curiosity, intuition, and inner knowing helped me overcome my fear. I became fearless as I never avoided life's challenges, which helped me arrive at that state of knowingness. Tell you that this knowingness is very gratifying and pleasing. Anyone can achieve that state of knowingness after knowing reality. You, too, can see the truth if you dare to rebel against the established social system and question the truthfulness of the dogmas.

....

Greta Thunberg rebelled against the establishment. She even challenged the governments of the earth and market forces simply because she was attuned to her 'real nature,' her "true self", and sensed the lurking destruction of climate change. Her passionate call is being heard internationally. People from every corner of the globe wait for Fridays when millions of schoolchildren fill the streets in every country. Surprisingly, elders are joining them, putting the governments and super-rich in the lurch and anxious. Her passion for climate activism began at a young age. Greta first encountered the issue of climate change at 8 years old. As she learned more, her concerns deepened. She discovered that carbon dioxide (CO2) was a major contributor to global warming, often released by air travel. Despite many people acknowledging the seriousness of the climate crisis, they continued to worsen it by frequently flying for vacations. This contradiction motivated Greta to take action. She fearlessly asks whether the actions promised by the governments of the Earth are being executed. She was greatly disturbed to find that there were only empty promises, one after another, and no significant action whatsoever was being accomplished. Governments everywhere were at the mercy of the corporate world. "Market forces," which are being controlled by the "invisible hands" of the corporate world, don't allow them to intervene in the affairs of the rich and mighty.

In 2002, Luiz Inácio Lula da Silva, the Brazilian president, won a significant victory with a promise to combat poverty and redistribute wealth. However, the challenges began immediately. Lula's party had outlined its goals in a document called "Another Brazil is Possible," including breaking free from IMF restrictions on economic policies. But before he even took office, Brazil faced a 30% currency devaluation, a significant outflow of funds, and the world's highest debt-risk ratings. Lula's aide, Frei Betto, lamented that they were in government but lacked true power. He pointed out that real power had shifted to global corporations and financial capital, a trend influenced by Adam Smith's 1776 book "Wealth of Nations." Smith's economic theories emphasised self-interest, free markets, and the "invisible hand" of the economy benefiting society. While well-intentioned, this shift allowed capitalism to exploit both people and the Earth's resources, resulting in greater wealth inequality and contributing to climate change.

The beauty of democracy is that it puts enormous power over the people. Whether it is a democracy or otherwise, the power of the people cannot be disputed. The difficulty is that people are not aware of their powers. No one ever imagined that an individual could bring the world together. And a great movement of people has started to stop the mindless exploitation of Mother Earth. It was no less than a miracle when on September 23, 2019, a 16-year-old climate activist Greta Thunberg stunned the world with her speech at the UN against the might of the governments of the earth and the corporate world. Thunberg's concern was the threat of "Climate Change 'Biggest Threat Modern Humans Have Ever Faced', World-Renowned Naturalist Tells Security Council, Calls for Greater Global Cooperation." United Nations website. On a high level, the Security Council met on 23 February 2021. Naturalist David Attenborough warns that if we stay on our current path, we risk the collapse of essential aspects of our security, including food production, access to fresh water, habitable temperatures, and ocean food chains. This threat could lead to the breakdown of civilization, particularly affecting the poorest and most vulnerable. Attenborough emphasizes our duty to help those in immediate danger and suggests that developing skills among the less fortunate could be a beneficial approach.

....

Skill development is much more vital than any other teaching. Especially for the poor who do not know where their next meal will come from. Training them to grow their own food can revolutionise their lives. It is not a difficult task. They can be trained in the skill in a few days. They can grow vegetables, herbs, beans, and even a few fruits using the soilless water-based hydroponic farming and/ or 'Growbag' farming systems. Since these crops can be harvested at home - even indoors, grow light can be used for indoor plants. Growing and consuming their own uncooked live foods would make them healthy and disease-free. When they are healthy, other expenses would be negligible: medical expenses, cooking fuel expenses, reduced shopping frequency, and other expenses will result in savings. Besides, they can sell or barter if they produce more than their requirements. That will ensure their independence. Besides, they can offer their services to people who want to grow their own vegetables.

The consequences will be far-reaching if a large world population consumes plant-based, uncooked and/or lightly cooked foods. Many food-producing, packaging, and transport industries that emit lots of CO2 into the environment - will be made redundant. Less use of these gas-guzzling industries and vehicles means reduced discharge of CO2 and reduced environmental pollution. That is needed to control climate change and save humanity from going extinct. Raw foods are of higher quality, requiring less consumption to meet nutritional needs. Cooking heat can deplete vitamins, damage proteins and fats, and destroy digestion-enhancing enzymes. Increasing the proportion of raw foods in your diet can leave you feeling satisfied with more energy from smaller meals, thanks to the optimal water balance in raw food.

Additionally, eating raw can save you money on food, vitamins, cookware, medical expenses, and health insurance. More than often, articles advocate for a diet rich in whole, fresh, and raw fruits, nuts, and vegetables, which are teeming with life and can impart their vitality directly to you. When you can stay 100% healthy by consuming raw live food without cooking, why waste time and precious money on energy-guzzling kitchen devices? The average U.S. residential home consumed approximately 10,399 kilowatt-hours (kWh) of electricity per year in 2017, translating to an average of 867 kWh per month. This means the daily average household electricity consumption is around 28.9 kWh (867 kWh / 30 days). It's important to consider the environmental impact of such electricity consumption in the U.S. and around the world, especially given the use of appliances that contribute to CO2 emissions.

Over the years, excessive reliance on fossil fuels, including coal, natural gas, crude oil, and others, has led to significant environmental consequences, such as air and water pollution and global warming. As pointed out in the article "Fossil Fuels: The Dirty Facts" by Malissa Denchak, the problem is substantial and demands an urgent solution.

One way to address these challenges is by recognizing the "law of divine oneness," which underpins the universal laws. This law emphasises the interconnectedness of all things in creation. As Jessica Estrade highlights in her article "How to Harness the Power of the 12 Laws of the Universe To Improve Your Life," every action we take has a ripple effect that impacts not only ourselves but also the collective. It serves as a reminder that our actions matter and can make a positive difference.

That means our excessive energy consumption has a ripple effect and impacts the collective – it impacts not only ourselves but also the universe, including humanity and Mother Earth. We have been over consuming energy for the last several decades and have caused enormous harm to our health and the health of Mother Nature.

As mentioned earlier, Einstein's wisdom reminds us that everything in existence is energy. To achieve the reality we desire, we must align with its frequency. This principle applies not only to our thoughts and intentions but also to everything we consume, as all things, whether food, goods, or resources, are ultimately composed of energy. Consumption of things in moderation is not harmful, but we create a problem when we consume excessively. Our carbon footprint is a measure of our energy consumption activity. The average carbon footprint for a person in the United

States is 16 tons, one of the highest rates in the world, whereas "Global experts call for a target limit of approximately 2 tonnes per person per year."

The average carbon footprint of Americans is too high, but developed countries along with some high-income oil-producing developing countries have the highest emissions per capita. Almost all are above the global average. But in developing countries, the carbon footprint of the high-income group is no less. Unconsciously, we all consume enormous energy by consuming consumer goods excessively, whether food or non-food items or consumer goods. Excessive consumer goods also mean excessive consumption of transportation services because consumer goods need to be transported.

Our escalating demand for raw materials has surged over the years, tripling our natural resource consumption between 1970 and 2010. However, this excessive consumption exacerbates climate issues, intensifies air pollution, and strains our planet's life-sustaining systems, including those that supply fresh water and essential materials crucial for our well-being.

The solution is obvious: we must reduce our energy consumption. The real problem, however, is that people are not aware that they are over consuming energy. Unaware, they are digging their own graves through this self-destructive behaviour – Ignorance isn't always bliss. The solution is nothing but to remove ignorance and make people aware of the truth by being trustworthy by unveiling the facts of life and decoding the puzzles of life.

CHAPTER NINE

HUMANISM

The American Humanist Association defines Humanism as a progressive life philosophy that emphasises ethical living and the greater good without relying on theism or supernatural beliefs. Regarding the question of serving the greater good, it involves choosing actions that benefit many, showing selflessness, engaging in charity, and sometimes making personal sacrifices for the sake of others and the future well-being of humanity. In essence, it means being compassionate and aspiring to better the world beyond oneself.

Compassion is essential, as articulated in Berth A. Lown's article titled "Compassion Is a Necessity and an Individual and Collective Responsibility." She explains that compassion is a complex trait influenced by various factors, including individual characteristics, immediate surroundings, societal norms, and organisational culture. Compassion serves as an ethical foundation in healthcare, not a luxury, and it is a widely held value. Removing barriers to compassion among healthcare professionals can mitigate burnout, enhance their well-being, and contribute to achieving the goal of improving patient care experiences while reducing costs. This doesn't only apply to healthcare professionals. I see youngsters unable to decide when to push on in their jobs and stride further in their careers, and when they need a break. Only a senior's compassion and guidance can help them identify this distinction to create a healthy life.

"Compassion Is a Necessity and an Individual and Collective Responsibility." It means having a love for Humanity is innate. We lack knowledge about our actual being; we are divided between our true selves and ego selves. Eliminate the ego; we feel an immediate connection with our true selves. The true self is the embodiment of love and compassion, and humanness.

In their book "The Origin of Humanness is in the Biology of Love," Humberto Maturana Romesín and Gerda Verden-Zöller argue that humanness is rooted in the biology of love. They propose that our species has evolved by prioritising love and cooperation expressed through emotions like mutual respect, care, acceptance, and trust (Homo sapiens-amans) rather than competition and aggression (Homo sapiens aggression or arrogance). This perspective situates ethics within biology, as a responsible concern for the well-being of others naturally emerges from living with the principles of love. This approach offers hope for a cultural change away from domination and control, emphasising the importance of embracing the biology of love and intimacy as our foundation for a more compassionate society.

And don't forget that human "cells are human beings", and compassion is innate in them too. The biology of love and intimacy extends even to the cellular level. In her article "Biology of Love – What can our cells tell us about the importance of love," Carol Dixon explores this connection. Dr. Bruce Lipton, a stem cell biologist and author of "The Biology of Belief," describes it as the "Honeymoon Effect." During this passionate phase of life, our perception of the world expands, and we radiate delight, not limited to our partners but embracing life itself.

Remarkably, every one of our cells behaves like a miniature human, according to Lipton. Inside us, fifty trillion human-like cells collaborate to perform essential functions like pumping the heart and breathing. When we experience being "in love," our cells resonate with the vibration of love. It's a profound connection between our emotional state and our cellular biology.

"The cell (from Latin cella, meaning - small room) is the basic structural, functional, and biological unit of all known organisms. A cell is the smallest unit of life. Cells are often called the" building blocks of life ." The study of cells is called cell biology, cellular biology, or cytology.," writes Dr: Fadia Al-khayat in her article "Cell and Molecular Biology." That means 30/40 trillion cells of our body are a conscious unit of life and charged with love. Even though they are in great numbers, their love for life and each other holds them and the body of the colony together. Because they all have the same purpose - to work hard for the greater good of the colony called the body; altruistically, that is nothing but doing good to Humanity. They have to because they exist or survive when the body exists and is healthy. Humans, too, are biological entities and are not devoid of the biology of love. Instead, ethics and love are situated in their biology. Inherently they have the urge to do great good to Humanity. That is their fundamental reality.

Naturally, there is a yearning to do the greater good or serve humanity. The reality is that cells are children of a colony called the body - the human body - and love for the human body is situated in them. Likewise, humans are children of Mother Earth, and love for Mother Earth is situated in them. It is in their drive to serve the body of Mother Nature to preserve its green cover. It is their essential need and requirement for their life. They cannot survive without the green surface of planet Earth, from which they get all their nourishment because Nutrients are chemical substances found in every living thing on Earth. Therefore, to keep themselves alive and healthy, they must preserve their green cover and keep it free from hazards.

And when we remember that "love" is situated in our "biology", it becomes only a matter of finding our fundamental reality. According to Deepak Chopra, the "fundamental reality is in the field of awareness". We miss this reality and miss understanding our true selves because we are not aware of our core selves. Our true selves are nothing but our fundamental reality which many would also understand as the ultimate truth or our awareness. Unaware of these realities, of our true selves can cause disorder internal as well as external. In the lack of self-awareness, we made ourselves perennially sick. When we are not entirely physically, mentally, emotionally, and spiritually healthy, I believe that we are sick. We are sick when we miss reality; our mood is downbeat, and our thoughts are sluggish. The root cause is we are the victim of our ego-self. More than often, we are highly engaged with our ego-self. Our ego-self, stunned by beautiful stories narrated by the world, doesn't get time to give attention to the fundamental realities of life, the field of awareness causing disorder in life and chaos everywhere. Your life is cluttered with unnecessaries. You're confused and unbalanced. And the only way to regain your awareness is to become self-aware. Every Time you cleaned your room, and threw away things you didn't need, it helped you become more aware of how you have grown as a person, and what is necessary to you.   Regain because you lost your authentic self in the free-for-all of life, and what is lost can be retrieved. Unconsciously we seek that reality because we are the summation of all humanity, wherever we live. We are the representatives of every human being. It needs to be regained and it can be that we only need to jog our memories.

....

Biofield science is a growing field of research. According to Karen L. Dean's article, it explores the human biofield, often called the "energy field" or "living matrix." This biofield integrates the functions within an organism, connecting them to both its energetic and physical environment. It extends beyond the body, facilitating subtle exchanges between individuals and their surroundings.

Another emerging field is the study of emotions in biology. Scientists suggest that emotions evolved to aid survival in higher organisms. However, issues with the biological systems regulating emotions, such as major depression or chronic anxiety, can make daily survival more challenging, as noted by Huda Akil, PhD, in her article "The Biology of Love."

In "Molecules of Emotion," Candace B. Pert explores the fascinating connection between emotions and biology. She unveils a pivotal concept: peptides in our bodies serve as the molecules of emotion, significantly influencing how our body and mind interact. These molecules can trigger various physical reactions and even mobilise our immune system to combat threats like tumours. Pert's mission goes beyond her scientific discoveries. She aims to bridge the gap between complex research and everyday understanding. Her goal is to make this knowledge practical and accessible to everyone.

Central to her work is the concept of the biofield, which enables the subtle exchange of emotional patterns between individuals and their environment. In simple terms, our emotional states have a profound impact not only on ourselves but also on the world around us. Positive emotions radiate positivity, while negativity can create a ripple effect of negativity. In essence, Candace B. Pert's research highlights the powerful interplay between emotions, biology, and the biofield, emphasising how our emotional well-being can influence both our personal lives and the broader world.

Electronic media, through which information arrives everywhere in the world and changes the pattern in human behaviour. It is not limited to a local assemblage. Its reach has become possible to the whole world. Through the media, this is not limited, but the whole world is affected. Today we can see through different media – television, radio, and newspapers -   that almost every country in the world is hostile to other countries, creating a hostile pattern and causing anxiety worldwide. Even more worrying is corporate behaviour. They have been causing a negative pattern through their inaccurate advertisements for the last several decades by putting ignorant people in an unreasonable, unrealistic, purposeless competitive mode which creates a hostile pattern worldwide, and peace is missing from the surface of the planet Earth. Often internships and first jobs instil this behavioural change in individuals.

In the article "Humans' Natural State is Peace, Not Violence," Jeremy Pollack challenges the notion that the world is becoming more violent. He acknowledges the perception of increased violence, driven by media coverage of mass shootings, warfare, and aggression. However, Pollack argues that studies suggest violence levels haven't necessarily risen but that our increased media exposure to such events creates the impression of increased violence in the world.

Today the entire world competes and when there is competition, there is fear of losing; and competition creates an interference pattern in our biofield, causing hostility toward each other. Today the whole world is creating that interference. No one seems to be at peace. The whole world is sitting on a tinderbox, ready to explode anytime. People live in fear because they do not know the reality and run after a fantasy created by the invisible hands of market forces and profit-hungry media controlled by the super-rich.

The simplest way out would be to love yourself, love your cells, and care for your cells and your environment compassionately because cells prosper when you care for yourself and the environment. Listen to your gut. When cells prosper, you prosper. How can the trillions of cells take care of your body when you are not caring for yourself and the cells?   It will be gross negligence if you do not love your body and cells compassionately. And why you shouldn't make them healthy when it promises you a disease-free, immaculate healthy life. The only way left is for people to love themselves, love their cells, and love Mother Earth, which supports their lives.

....

"Everything is energy, and that's all there is to it. Match the frequency of the reality you want, and you cannot help but get that reality. It can be no other way. This is not philosophy. This is physics.," writes Diler Yazici in his article, "I say: "Everything in the universe is energy!" and Einstein confirms. Diler Yazici asserts that everything in the universe is energy and that matching the frequency of the desired reality is a fundamental principle. This idea, he states, isn't mere philosophy but physics. The universe comprises three types of energy: dark energy, dark matter, and normal matter. Dark energy and dark matter, though unseen, play crucial roles, with dark matter being particularly elusive to current detection methods.

Normal matter, which includes all observable living and non-living entities, is composed of atoms; these seemingly solid entities have hidden aspects. Some scientists are now exploring the notion of consciousness in matter and the entire universe. Corey S. Powell, a science writer, suggests that modern science has been bridging the gap between humans and the universe, emphasising our connection to the cosmos. Gregory Matloff's hypothesis introduces the idea of a "proto-consciousness field" extending through space, implying that the universe itself might possess self-awareness, challenging traditional perspectives on our place within it.

If so, the possibility of the cosmos having a creative mind cannot be invalidated. Assuming that the cosmos has a creative mind; it would be exciting to fancy the thoughts of a self-aware Cosmic

Mind. Possibly millions of years ago, the Cosmic Mind visualised creating an inspiring land of plenty with coral rugose rough-hewn mountains, and lush green forests, the expansive seas inhabited by millions of species. It gestated the idea for many, many million years before delivering an immaculate beautiful planet Earth, infused with all the laws of Nature. Trees, plants, flowers, and other species lived in perfect coordination, sharing and using minimum energy to ward off any threat to the globe's ecology as per the laws of Nature and kept it unspoiled for thousands and thousands of years. All beings struggled and co-existed for a few millennia. Then hominids (apes) evolved into bipedal animals. Bipedalism allowed hominids to free their arms, allowing them to walk on two legs, become self-aware, and use tools. Hominids evolved into intelligent homo sapiens, who developed language, music, religion, etc. As the thinking mind of humans evolved further, communities developed. Each community developed its own culture, and conflict between cultures became common. Though cultures fought between themselves for dominance, security, and survival, they didn't harm the natural beauty of Mother Earth.

Then, a few hundred years ago, the devil appeared with the facade of capitalism.   I have expanded more on Capitalism in the next chapter. Anyway, capitalists didn't regard the laws of Nature and started hurting the loving fabric of the earth. They have begun to exploit the earth's natural resources and the resources of innocent humans to accumulate wealth and more wealth. This unethical practice spread to all parts of the globe as time passed. But for governments, regulations restricted them from exploiting disproportionately. I blame the capitalists' "love for money" turning into greed after the publication of Adam Smith's book, "Wealth of Nations", in 1776. This turned the table in favour of the capitalists. Ethical use of capitalism became lessons that remained in the business schools and university books.

My cherished daughters, in today's consumer-focused world, it's vital to maintain our ethical values. We must delve deep within ourselves and strive to preserve the essence of humanity in this corporate-driven society. Being consciously ethical means making choices aligned with our values, even when it's tough. As we navigate this capitalist landscape, let us lead by example, showing that ethics and humanity endure.

CHAPTER TEN

CONSUMERISM

The capitalists got a legitimate way to dupe their customers through the "invisible hands" of "market forces" that Adam Smith promoted and got recognition for. The core of Smith's thesis was that humans' natural tendency toward self-interest (or, in modern terms, looking out for yourself) results in prosperity. Smith argued that by giving everyone the freedom to produce and exchange goods as they pleased (free trade) and opening the markets up to domestic and foreign competition, people's natural self-interest would promote greater prosperity than with stringent government regulations," writes Joy Blenman in his article titled "Adam Smith and The Wealth of Nation." "This free-market force became known as the invisible hand, but it needed support to bring about its magic. The automatic pricing and distribution mechanisms in the economy—which Adam Smith called an "invisible hand"—interacted directly and indirectly with centralised, top-down planning authorities. However, there are some meaningful conceptual fallacies in an argument that is framed as the invisible hand versus the government." This is how we lose our connection to our true selves. We are no longer aligned with our cosmic mind, true selves as we were before capitalism's appearance, which gave birth to consumerism. I believe that consumerism is the root cause of all crises including "global warming", "climate change", and "climatic disruption", as well as "environmental destruction", "weather destabilisation", and "environmental collapse".

Freed from government regulation, global corporations got a free hand. Their self-interest turned into voracious avarice in the 20th century, and there has been a rise in plundering the earth's resources. A report from the UN Environment Programme's International Resource Panel reveals that the growing middle class has led to a significant increase in resource extraction, going from 22 billion tonnes in 1970 to 70 billion tonnes in 2010. This rise in consumption is driven by a culture of consumerism, particularly in the 21st century, which encourages people to buy more and more goods and services.

Mass production during the Industrial Revolution contributed to overproduction, where supply exceeded demand. To combat this, manufacturers started using planned obsolescence and persuasive advertising to boost consumer spending. Thus, unethical practices got a wing. Business houses used fake but beautiful stories to market their goods and services. They were fake because they never revealed the truth, the unpleasantness that each mass-produced good or service engenders. The factories emit a massive amount of CO_2 and pollute the environment triggering climate change. They sold the products with the magical power of words - advertisements - they camouflaged the reality behind charming words. They created a culture of consumerism based on false assurances, far from the truth, using persuasive effective words in the advertisement which affected consumer behaviour. I, myself have observed this behaviour of false advertising among my social circle. It isn't an uncommon practice. On the other hand, consumers become crazy for the offerings that devoid them of their critical thinking power - an invaluable gift of evolution to human beings. But for them, immediate gratification seems more important than anything else.

Natasha Levis claims that the 1920s brought mass production, expanding markets, and innovations. This era marked a surge in personal prosperity and improved living standards. With consumers having more money, manufacturers aimed to persuade them to purchase even unnecessary products, a new challenge. They didn't care to tell the reality that every product and service that is being mass-produced leaves a massive amount of carbon footprint and adds to climate change - a dire threat to humanity. They used the words – ads - as a weapon to mislead ignorant consumers by hiding the repulsive stories, hidden behind their products. They knew that customers wouldn't fall for the product if they knew the reality hidden behind their beautifully worded, inaccurate stories.

Slowly but with certainty, many global corporations kept accumulating wealth, leaving the poor at the mercy of gods and Mother Nature in despair. Their insatiable greed for money has no end. They gathered the treasures as if they would carry their riches to enjoy the afterlife, just as Pharaohs got buried in pyramids with all the wealth they amassed during their lifetime. Their charity organisations ran for profit. Their welfare schemes were misplaced. Even their drugs made people sicker, causing drug industry burgeons, a source of making, unethical money. Even during the Pandemic, which made people jobless and the poor poorer, they found ways to convince the masses to accumulate more wealth. When the world economy went from bad to worse, the stock market soared while people suffered extensively worldwide; they were too busy building up their possessions.

The greater evil was that all the governments of the earth were not free to work for the good of their citizenry as promised in their manifestos when it went against the market forces controlled by the invisible hand of the corporate world. In the electoral system of democracies, the politicians needed lots of money for their campaigns to fight the election. They were no more than puppets, the strings held by market forces controlled by capitalists, and these kinds of money never come without a bargain. There are instances where governments with all the good intentions of improving the sorry state of the oppressed couldn't turn their program promised in their manifestoes to the people as it frustrated the interests of global corporations. Resultant, people never got the kind of good dividend they had the right to.

Indifferent to the suffering of millions, we must confront a grim reality: about 4 billion people live in Tier 4 at the bottom of the economic pyramid, with an annual per capita income below $1,500. Shockingly, over a billion people, roughly one-sixth of the world's population, survive on less than $1 per day. Moreover, the income gap between the rich and poor continues to widen. In 1960, the wealthiest 20 per cent of the world's population accounted for about 70 per cent of total income, a figure that swelled to 85 per cent by 2000. In contrast, the poorest 20 per cent saw their share of global income dwindle from 2.3 per cent to a mere 1.1 per cent, according to the United Nations.

To address this disparity, people worldwide must awaken the "Man the Reformer" within themselves. The path to change lies within, where dormant reformers await activation. We all possess the precious gift of human potentiality, and it's within our power to make a difference. It is disgraceful for us humans not to be aware of the limitless potentiality of our consciousness. We missed this most valuable aspect of life. Almost the whole world missed this fact. There would not have been so much anguish and devastation in the world had we been aware of the powers of our true selves. We all had always felt that there was something wrong. Always our true self nudged us whenever we were faulted. But the rot is so deeply rooted that the voice of pure self has become very feeble. Our recognition of our own frailty should not be underestimated, as it has resulted in significant harm. It is imperative, that we evolve into resolute reformers because, as Emerson so aptly put it, the purpose of life extends beyond mere happiness. Instead, it entails being of service, maintaining honour, displaying compassion, and leaving a meaningful legacy through a well-lived and virtuous existence.

Nearly the entire world is the victim of their self-centred, most evil scheme. They knew that if the consumer came to see the reality, they wouldn't be able to sell their product by revealing the truth. That meant "sawing off the branch they are sitting on!" a recipe for destroying the wealth they have been hoarding for a long time. Had the people been told the truth, hid behind their fictitious narratives and taught the lesson of humanness and dependency of life on the naturalness of earth, the plundering would have stopped many decades back. People are conditioned to think that material possessions are essential in life, without which happiness cannot be achieved. That was enough to put people in an unmindful, unending rat race for wealth, the kind of race the super-rich already were/are in. In that foolhardy race, both of them - the global corporations and consumers – missed the values of life and remained no more than a "rat" even if they won the race". Both were running after an unreal mirage forgetting everything that matters, a "loving humanness".

In their mad race, the transnational corporations stripped the earth bare to its bones. The world's governments, shareholders, managers, executives, traders, and many more saw the disrobing of the planet but remained silent for fear of the invisible hand of market forces. They couldn't dare to speak the truth against them, which were controlled by market forces and the invisible hands of Global corporations. A 16-year-old girl, Greta Thunberg, saw their evil design and rose from the ashes like a phoenix to resurrect the vigorous people of their stupor to re-robe the earth. She dared and challenged people who thought themselves mightier than the gods. Her challenge brought millions of children to the streets all over the world. Those 'gods of words' sitting at a dizzying height - a height from where there is an un-scalable void if they look up and climb down are perilous. Thanks to Greta, they are confused, and their fall is as inevitable as Humpty Dumpty's fall.

Neglecting the impact of others' misfortune is a missed chance for a profound shift in our perspective. Daisaku Ikeda reminds us that our happiness is linked to the happiness of others. It's crucial to see ourselves in others and foster unity. Discriminating against others is, essentially, discrimination against ourselves, and causing harm to others ultimately harms us. Conversely, showing respect to others enhances our own lives. Consumers were deceived by persuasive words, believing products met their needs, unaware of the deception Schools, instead of teaching life's realities, focused on competition. Governments, elected for their people's welfare, conspired with capitalists, amassing wealth while neglecting education.

Global corporations' misplaced priorities and government education policies have brought us to a critical point. If governments were truthful and corporations honest, we'd have harmony. Sadly, they've indulged in animalistic instincts, creating global crises. Urgent action is needed to save humanity.

....

Authors gain valuable insights when writing their books due to extensive research. In an interview about his book "God: A Story of Revelation," Deepak Chopra was asked about the impact of the writing process on his faith and the lessons he learned. Chopra shared that the most significant lesson was the realisation that many of the profound questions we ask today, like our origins, the existence of God, the nature of the soul, and what happens after death, have been pondered for centuries. He marvelled at the historical depth of human inquiry and the intelligence reflected in past answers to these questions.   In historical times, intelligent people deliberated on such non-material questions, from which came the idea of God, and everyday people accepted the idea. People "believed in an afterlife eternity, which penetrated almost every culture. Their temporary life didn't matter much; it was a preparation for the afterlife." Says Amany Fawzy. Living a fulfilling life has long been associated with practising virtues like kindness, humility, wisdom, and honesty. These values create a recipe for happiness, as highlighted by Derrick Carpenter. This idea has endured for thousands of years. Critical thinking, too, has ancient roots. Socrates, as recorded by Plato, is one of the earliest proponents of critical thinking. He emphasised the need to question those in authority, recognizing that power and position don't necessarily equate to sound knowledge. Socrates stressed the importance of probing deeply into our thoughts before accepting ideas as valid beliefs. But that habit of depending on authority continues and persists even now.

In John Antonakis' article on power and corruption, echoing John Emerich Edward Dalberg-Acton, it's emphasised that power tends to corrupt, especially absolute power. Multinational Corporations (MNCs) wield significant global influence, often shaping governments' decisions. Noam Chomsky also underscores MNCs' role, labelling them the modern "masters of mankind." These corporations have a history of exploiting resources and people, resembling a "greed virus." Adam Smith's concept of masters of humankind should have been about promoting human welfare and love instead of this virus. The greed virus initially spread slowly but gained momentum in the last seven to eight decades. Masters' aggressive campaigns infected the world, turning it into a wealth-addicted society. Those infected became selfish and indifferent to the suffering of the poor.

People at the top of the economic pyramid could have alleviated poverty and prevented climate change but were blinded by their absolute power. They indulged in "guilty pleasure" and "big splurge," evading responsibility with their wealth and media savvy. The greed virus spread beyond conglomerates, infecting people worldwide who amassed money through unethical means. Both sought validation for their extravagant lifestyles, whether from the world or their communities. Guilt was overshadowed by ego, fear of giving up luxury, and facing problems tied to their ill-gotten wealth. These egocentric kings, falsely bedazzled, were seen as global saviours. People blindly accepted their offerings, unaware of the ugly reality behind them. The world suffered poverty and climate change due to the greed virus and the maxim "all for ours and nothing for others," followed religiously by these elites. Their behaviour, accumulating wealth regardless of fairness or foul means, led to cultural conflicts and wars they profited from. The general population suffered, causing mass migrations and hunger. Ending conflicts by ceasing weapons supply was unthinkable, as it would erode their wealth.

Critical thinking is the result of challenging the accepted idea. In olden times ordinary people dared not challenge themselves for fear of the unknown future or afterlife dilemma, which became a habit. But it is surprising that, even though the number of critical thinkers has risen, most people, including the educated, are not scientific thinkers. And the responsibility squarely goes on the marketers that play with words and stories – global corporations. For their self-interest, these industries took a free ride on the ordinary people by hiding the truth behind their alluring but nefarious stories, which snatched the power of making reasoned judgments and caused catastrophic damage to the global environment. All their products leave an enormous carbon footprint by the time they arrive at the consumers' doorstep, bringing the danger of extinction of humanity closer. Scientists warn that climate crises could cause untold suffering to societies if proper steps are not taken immediately, but they go unheeded.

....

Dr Tasha Eurich's research found that 10 to 15% of people are self-aware. That research was done on job performance. But what about the self-awareness of commonplace everyday people all over the world? I believe that their self-awareness must be insignificant. Thanks to systematic ignorance around us also marketed to parents and the faulty education system, every individual lives in a bubble of 'just enough'. People at large,   I believe, are not conscious of these incredible gifts of self-awareness.

Self-awareness makes people think about everything critically. Critical thinker engages in continuous self-reflection, closely monitoring their thoughts and emotions. This process involves active thinking, which entails problem-solving, and passive thinking, which involves applying learned thoughts and actions from previous experiences, as explained in the article "Mind Games: Active vs Passive Thinking" by Nights Staff. Conclusion: critical thinkers constantly observe their thoughts and feelings and take responsibility for their actions. It analyses them and makes changes. Just watch your feelings when you are sad. You will find that you are thinking about a hopeless event or situation. Just change your thoughts and think about a pleasant situation. Immediately your mood will change.

If you are not an active thinker, your thoughts limit you. You won't have the pluck to break the rules you have made around you. You are pleased with what charms you and try not to read between the lines. You believe everything literally. That is what people around the globe are doing—accepting stories offered by business houses without trying to know the reality. Beautiful amusing stories are woven around you and me since we are the targeted consumers. People fall for it because they do not know the unpleasantness concealed behind the shiny and attractive packaging with appealing promotional words.

If you think critically, you will find that all products offered by big business houses – whatever genre they fall under – are highly unhealthy, directly or indirectly. They are harmful when you consume them. Focus on the ingredients closely. Follow the manufacturing process. You will learn the truth. Besides, they generate enormous pollution in the environment and cause warming of the globe. You are a citizen of that, ultimately adversely affecting your health and the health of the planet Earth.

If you are an active thinker, you will think critically before consuming. You try hard to understand whether the product offered is good for you, your health, and the world; if the consumption of the goods and services harms you and humanity, you won't consume them or curtail their consumption. Avoid consuming anything that harms your health or the natural surroundings. The physical environment, which encompasses elements like air, trees, water bodies, and more, significantly affects the well-being of communities. Worldwide, People are being held captive by the grand tempting schemes plotted by the mega-rich, sitting in their opulent boardrooms, brainstorming how to hoodwink innocent consumers; the leitmotif of their stories - ad blitz - is a "sustained attack on consumers". How to make "customers feel like a king" and how not to displease them. Say nothing that may displease them; their charming stories send the customers into a frenzy that makes them crazy to buy their products or services. They have no idea that they are being betrayed. They have no idea that their unmindful behaviours are harming their health and the health of the physical environment they live in.
"

Customer is king" and "customer is always right" are the buzzwords in modern marketing. These are the magic mantras of the corporate world, which has built factories with large capacities to produce goods in huge quantities. Mass-produced goods need a large number of customers from all over the world. Their strategy has been an enormous success and their wealth increased by leaps and bounds. When consumers are treated like kings, their spending also multiplies. Their ad blitz blinds them. It makes customers crazy. Intoxicated by marketers' praises, consumers don't even realise that they have been celebrated like the allegorical king who got lost in honour of his invisible mantle by his courtesans. Who didn't know that he was made to wear nothing?

It is said that violent language kills the human spirit. But the words of appreciation masked with malcontent kill the human spirit even more masterfully. That's what marketers have been doing, killing the spirit of consumers all over the world by weaving beautiful but phoney stories to dodge them. The story is so winsome and fascinating that it spellbinds consumers. Consumers are told what they want to hear. They feel like a 'king'. Regrettably, the so-called king doesn't possess the characteristics of a king's energy. Though the consumers feel like a king, it miss the attributes of the king in all their fullness because it know nothing about the truth – the hard truth.

In the article "The Four Archetypes of the Mature Masculine: The King" on the "Art of Manliness" website, the King archetype is described. When a man embodies the King archetype, he possesses a deep inner confidence and purpose that provides balance and stability. He remains composed and in control even amidst chaos, taking proactive actions rather than reacting impulsively. He serves as a steadfast anchor during crises and maintains a broad perspective on situations, remaining unshaken by passing and superficial matters. This is the opposite of what a consumer truly is. Individuals are falsely treated as kings to buy into the products and further still lifestyle and beliefs of the industry. If consumers do not have enough to buy the product, financial assistance is facilitated for buying on instalments arranged - another way of cheating consumers. And the consumer is lured into buying more even if it is not a critical need for him. Attractive offers like "buy one get one free" are another way to cheat them. Many of us recognize that nothing is genuinely free. Corporations don't provide deals solely out of generosity; they do it because it benefits their business. In some cases, these promotions can be misleading, as pointed out by Zachary Crockett in the article on the questionable economics of "buy one get one free" offers. They are never made aware of the unpleasant truth behind the story. They are not aware that the mass-produced products have a depressing tale. They are unaware that every such product adds to global warming, ultimately a health hazard for all. The knowledge could make customers rethink postpone, or even cancel their intent to purchase that product. Another way of cheating is that the products have an expiry date or go kaput in a set time frame that requires a replacement that keeps their factories from going idle, another way of multiplying their wealth.

This world has become an Orwellian society.   I say "Orwellian" because as   George Orwell identified, it is a situation, idea, as well as a societal condition that is destructive to the welfare of a free and open society. The Orwellian speech says, "Doublespeak is the language that deliberately obscures, disguises, distorts, or reverses the meaning of words. Doublespeak may take the form of euphemisms (e.g., "downsizing" for layoffs and "servicing the target" for bombing), in which case it is primarily meant to make the truth sound more palatable". In this age of the internet, you have no privacy. The big bosses are watching you closely. The internet, smart mobiles and artificial intelligence have made possible constant surveillance of consumers by the big bosses. Unaware, you are remote-controlled, and you are doing exactly what the big fish want you to do, slowly emptying your bank balance by captivating you with fake stories and false promises. The entire study of marketing focuses on wielding powerful stories (albeit, ethically inside a classroom) to ensure a sale.   "The most important factor is enthusiasm. Bring out the fear, the surprise, the sheer joy — all of those emotions are what keep the reader engaged," writes Sean D'Souza in his article, "How to Weave a Story that Instantly Captivates Your Audience". They never tell the horrid account that the product carries with it. The production processes and transportation cause enormous damage to the environment and our health. The stories are so absorbing that their magic overpowers consumers - it sends them into a hypnotic spell, making them go head over heels to buy the product. Capitalists never let the unpleasant hard truth surface. They know that the knowledge of reality would provoke the minds of the consumers. And, a critical reason wouldn't buy the product without going into the nitty-gritty of the products.

It is a travesty and tragedy that neither the corporate biggies nor the customers possess the fullness of a king. The difference is that the first, in all its probability, know what the 'king's fullness' is, but the fear of falling from grace makes them hold the truth back; a little of their courage could have been an attempt in a direction that would have paved the way for making the world a beautiful place for all. And, the customers, who primarily do not know anything about the "king's fullness", would be glad to join a mission after being made conscious of what the behaviour of the king's fullness is and how developing such behaviour can help make the world a better place for all.

CHAPTER ELEVEN

HIGHER CONSCIOUSNESS

Authenticity involves genuinely expressing your true self and emotions instead of presenting a facade. To achieve authenticity, you must first understand your genuine self. This authenticity, coupled with honesty and pursuing your passions, can elevate your consciousness beyond basic instincts, a characteristic unique to humans due to their advanced thinking capabilities. Higher consciousness is supposed to be the domain of spiritualism and is believed to be hard to experience. People, for thousands of years, thought that only spiritualists could experience higher consciousness. Thus the higher consciousness remained elusive in the lives of everyday people. Only a handful of privileged – true godmen - enjoyed the higher consciousness. Godmen did not care to impart that knowledge to everyday people truthfully. Perhaps because their place of worship needed disciples, they created a sphinx-like enigma around them that would attract people for their blessings. People were made to believe that higher consciousness is enigmatic and mysterious, and only godmen have the power to venture there. That belief took root in people's cultures and societies which were handed down. That culture penetrated every age, and it still prevails in every section of society in one form or the other worldwide. These cultures conditioned people's minds, which continues even today, and higher consciousness is still considered a distant unachievable dream.

I believe that this claim lacks truthfulness because anyone having common sense can elevate his awareness and achieve higher consciousness. It is only a matter of levels of awareness. According to Deepak Chopra, there are three levels of awareness: contracted awareness, expanded awareness, and pure awareness; with experience, your awareness moves from contracted to expanded awareness to pure awareness. The first level "is the level of problems, obstacles, and struggle." At level second, "solutions begin to appear." The third level "is the level where no problems exist." At the third level, you experience pure consciousness. It is your pure self and the only way to arrive at the level is by working towards self-awareness. You are already aware of your being, your surroundings, what is right, wrong, and the truth, and what is not. But you aren't self-aware. Not as yet. Often, when faced with hardship you withdraw into silence. The silence allows you to go into the recesses of your true self – higher consciousness – and you most often get the solution though you are not aware where you got the solution. But when you are self-aware you will be aware of all the levels of awareness. You will know that your higher consciousness is helping you.

How can you be self-aware? In everyday activities, you do not observe your mind's activities. You are aware in the simplest form, and don't give any attention to the sequence of activities taking place in your mind. You only need to be slightly more aware and push boundaries to observe the events taking place in your mind.

The thoughts, feelings, decisions, dreams, realisations, and conversations that are inert.   This particular awareness is self-awareness. You mindfully experience your thoughts and emotions and note how your true self is helping you. One way to arrive at it is to have "thoughtless awareness". In thoughtless awareness, "we have complete control over our minds". it seems quite impossible to arrive at a thoughtless state of mind. Though, unintentionally, you often go into thoughtless awareness. For example, when you do creative writing,   a form of artistic expression draws on the imagination to convey meaning through imagery, narrative, and drama there is no thought. You are free from thoughts; your mind is tranquil, and you see your inventive ideas clearly, just like in tranquil lake waters; you see the reflection of skies clearly, not in troubled waters. Self-awareness is practised in solitude or meditation. In solitude, you are calm and free from mental agitation, excitement, or disturbance, and you notice the feelings and emotions happening in your mind. In that state of mind, you experience higher consciousness.

To be dynamic in life, you need to be self-aware, "Self-awareness enables the whole mind-body system to be dynamic because self-awareness makes room for spontaneity, the exquisite freedom of the unexpected." – Deepak Chopra. Freedom from the unexpected means freedom from fear. Only human beings are endowed with this loving gift – higher consciousness. That is what distinguishes human beings from other creatures. Isn't it a matter of great anguish that people are unaware of their higher consciousness?   Unhappily I say this: you too, are not aware of your true self, of the pure self. You have yet to encounter your higher consciousness, although I can say that you may have peaked at it from a keyhole at certain points in life.

When you are aware of the individualities of your true self, you become self-aware. You were born honest, but you lost your honesty in the din of life. The good news is – what is lost can be reclaimed. Reclaiming your honesty means becoming aware of your true self, your cosmic mind. You need to find the course of action, to claim it back. It becomes easy to achieve your higher consciousness once you become aware of your true self. Children develop self-awareness in stages from birth to around age 4 or 5. Kendra Cherry, in her article on "Self-Awareness Development and Types," explains that self-awareness is evident in how children react to their own reflection in a mirror. It encompasses an awareness of various aspects of the self, such as traits, behaviours, and emotions. In essence, self-awareness is a psychological state where one becomes the primary focus of attention. Remember, you were more aware and more accurate to yourself during your academic period. Your character changed as you got influenced by the outer world. This isn't the point I draw your attention to; it is that you often change without noticing it. The root cause of all the world's troubles is that people haven't been able to free themselves from their conditioned minds. In the lack of higher consciousness, even the billionaires sitting on the top of the pyramid, considered the most influential and powerful individuals, haven't been able to do away with their conditioned minds.

During the whole term of your education in your boarding life, you naturally referred to your own spirit, to your true self. Regrettably, you were not aware that you were referring to your true self. Becoming self-aware through self-referral is key to understanding yourself deeply. In contrast, object referral leads to constant seeking of external approval and is fear-based. Knowing and comprehending your emotions, needs, and desires is a vital aspect of life, allowing you to lead an authentic, fulfilling, and joyful existence while maintaining your values and boundaries. This understanding also enables you to make informed, empathetic decisions, a crucial component of emotional intelligence. High EQ individuals excel in self-awareness, self-management, social awareness, and handling others' emotions. Self-aware people are cautious in their choices, considering their well-being and that of society. Human species all over the world possess the power of thinking and reasoning. This reasoning ability of humans separates us from all other species, and we humans can reason about everything before taking action. We, humans, can figure it out because we are bestowed with the power to refer to our true selves. That means all humans refer to themselves. The unfortunate thing is that we refer to ourselves unconsciously. And more distressing is that people who are aware of the potential of 'self' are few. Those few are trying their best to educate people about the presence and importance of true selves in their lives.

Heath Hilliard, in his article "Top 4 Traits of Self-Aware People," emphasises that self-awareness is your path to personal growth. He urges you to recognize your abilities and limitations, improve your self-awareness skills, and develop traits such as wisdom, honesty, humility, and confidence. The beauty of life as a human is that self-awareness can be cultivated, leading to a more genuine and happier life. In Caroline Forsey's article "Awareness (How to Tell if 'You're Actually Aware)," she defines self-awareness as your capacity to assess actions, thoughts, and emotions in alignment with internal standards. Highly self-aware individuals can objectively evaluate themselves, manage emotions, align behaviour with values, and comprehend how others perceive them. Being self-aware means understanding the profound influence of thoughts on actions, acknowledging that every effort's root lies in thoughts, and recognizing the law of "for every action, there is an equal opposite reaction." Your thoughts turn into the intention that engenders actions and reactions. Going to the market came first in your mind, which turned into physical activity. Thus the root of your actions arises from your thoughts. Mostly your actions are impulsive. But if you are a self-aware, critical thinker, you will take action only after analysing the probable consequence of your activity. You get feedback to know your mistakes and improve upon them.

All questions must be relational to your own existence - your total wellness - mind, body, and spirit. Remember, the answers to all your questions about existence lie within. You have to brainstorm with your 'Self' to find the answer. Brainstorming means you are thinking critically. You were a critical thinker when you wanted to perfect your hand in mastering a skill in academia - a game, painting, or writing up a poem. You can get the answer from other sources, but the final decision rests on how you utilise your critical thinking power.   People can shackle you physically, but they cannot imprison your thoughts. You, for some unknown, fear and have imprisoned your own views; you became uncritical; you feared criticising. Free them up from all conditioning and limitations. Hesitate not imagining the wildest dream you can dream of. Why fear? No one can peep into your mind,   your imagination! Your true self is your best friend.

You need to observe your thoughts come and go and weigh the consequences of your actions before taking action. You can decide in your thoughts whether to take action or not. You can weigh the probable impact of your actions before taking action. If your analytic mind reveals that your action's consequences could harm you and society, you will have the option of not taking the intended action. For example, you decided to buy a pack of potato chips. An investigation and analysis reveal that packaged potato chips harm your health because they are not fresh food. You also find that their production process and transportation generate too much CO_2 that pollutes the environment and causes a health hazard that ultimately affects your health and the health of society adversely.   Here you have two immediate choices, either proceed with purchasing and consuming the packet of chips or learn to avoid them. The latter is in tandem with self-consciousness. Your awareness may also have a ripple effect because you will warn others about the adverse impact of processed and packaged potato chips bought from the market. Every action of yours has ripple effects, within and without your body. Everything you do, every word you speak, and every action – thought action or otherwise - you make have a ripple effect on you and other people's lives.

Deep thinking, as explained by Dr. Jamie Schwandt, is the act of contemplating your own thinking process. René Descartes famously declared, "I think, therefore I am," emphasising the centrality of thought to human existence. This approach involves radical doubt, as Descartes questioned the certainty of everything, yet couldn't doubt the existence of the doubter, which was himself.

Embracing this doubting mindset is essential to becoming a deep thinker. You possess the ability to doubt your thoughts, and this self-awareness is crucial for personal growth.

Furthermore, your conscious awareness allows you to differentiate between your internal and external worlds. While conscious thoughts are within your awareness, subconscious processes occur beneath the surface. Sigmund Freud highlighted the tendency to repress unwanted thoughts and painful memories into the subconscious to avoid confronting them. This underscores the importance of doubting your thoughts and gaining control over your mind. By doing so, you enhance your critical thinking skills, creativity, and problem-solving abilities, ultimately helping you achieve both short-term and long-term goals.

Watch the chain of thoughts passing in your mind and the reactions each thought provokes, the way a character in movies is often seen having dialogue, with his own image mirrored in his mind's eyes. When you watch your thoughts, you know the content of your thoughts. Knowing the content is necessary because it remains for a fleeting second. When you know them, you can manage your thoughts. Managing your thoughts means eliminating unproductive thoughts. Thus your imaginative power grows. Your mind has the limitless power of imagination. You can learn to teach yourself with this exercise. Isn't it an embarrassment that you don't know your mind power? Almost the whole world believed in the divination of soothsayers and market forces and failed to know the reality of its limitless mental powers. They avoid the most commonsensical questions for fear of the unknown, even though they doubt their truthfulness. You were not always. You were a deep thinker in your days at your alma mater. To retrieve your thinking power, you must reclaim the true nature and freedom you enjoyed in your academic life. It would be best to question everything you see, hear, taste, smell, or feel.   You can doubt everything because everything is real for as long as your mind experiences it. Everything happens when you are mindful of the present moment. Everything becomes unreal when your mind is elsewhere.   Keep in mind that being fully present at the moment is essential, as the taste of food is truly experienced when your mind is focused on it, and you can only truly see what's in front of you when your awareness is engaged. Being present is the foundation of critical thinking. You must be aware of what is going on around and inside your mind, inside your body. You must be self-aware and start doubting everything.

Without critical thinking, we fall victim to the beautiful but fictitious word of praise – advertisements - global corporations bombard us by selling their unhealthy, useless products and services to multiply their fortune without regard for the consequences on consumers' health. They built their citadels on the misfortunes of everyday people.

We have arrived at this dire situation simply because we are not self-aware; people are not self-aware; they are ignorant. We are not aware that we have a cosmic mind. Even the super-rich aren't aware of their cosmic mind. In ignorance, we all are chasing a mirage. But they are ignorant. In their ignorance, they missed experiencing higher consciousness. An invaluable gift bestowed on all humans we are ignorant of. We all are ignorant, and in our ignorance, we allied with their evil plan and chased a mirage that cluttered our lives and minds with meaningless things.

CHAPTER TWELVE

CUT THE CLUTTER

"Anything that goes on in your mind is ripe to be 'clutter' if you haven't learned how to focus and organise internally," explains Craig Travis, PhD director of behavioural sciences at Ohio Health Grant Medical Center in Columbia, Ohio.

While being submerged in ignorance of what you truly are, you have involuntarily been impacted by external factors – that is – money, fame, grade, and praise. You, like most, raced after a never-ending unreal mirage and cluttered your mind and life with needless things.

People clean cookware before re-cooking, vacuum clean their houses often, and sanitise their bodies every day. It is worrisome that people don't think of decluttering their houses and minds with unnecessary things and thoughts. Cluttering one's space not only leads to confusion and indecision but also hampers one's ability to focus, affecting their productivity. Furthermore, clutter can have adverse effects on anxiety levels and sleep quality.

For instance, let' that your home contains an unnecessary accumulation of items mirroring the clutter in your thoughts. Look at the things you could do without but may strongly impact the life of your maid for the better.

The excessive collection contributes to the unequal distribution of wealth globally, with social and economic issues stemming from this disparity, as highlighted in "Rehabilitation Robotics." Problems such as poverty, hunger, homelessness, and environmental pollution all share the same root cause: the inequitable allocation of the world's wealth and resources. "The world holds enough for everyone's needs, but not everyone's greed," said Mahatma Gandhi, which is now one of his best-known quotes. Its ubiquity is for a good reason. Our 'must-have, must-buy' economy is eating into the planet's resources like never before, something Gandhi foresaw three-quarters of a century ago. He also warned us of the dangers of other countries taking to Western industrialism," writes Oliver Bach in an article, The Relevance of Gandhi in the Capitalism Debate, published in The Guardian. Setting distribution of wealth is hugely disproportionate, and it also robbed Mother Earth of its rich resources causing great harm to the environment and humanity.

By bringing up memories, decluttering makes us conscious of the consequences of wrongs committed to us, as well as those that we committed. It inspires us to correct the wrongs done. The process can be painful. As such, you need to be prepared for sadness and remorse. With perseverance, I feel sure that you will find the journey exciting. To begin with, you have two objectives: to discover your true potential and start cutting the clutter from your life and mind. You can kill two birds with one stone: 'minimalism'.

Joshua Fields, Millburn & Ryan Nicodemus founded "The Minimalist" website in 2010, attracting an audience of 20 million people. Their philosophy revolves around the idea that minimalism isn't solely about having less but creating space for more in life — more time, passion, creativity, experiences, contribution, contentment, and freedom. By decluttering your life from unnecessary possessions, you gain precious time to explore your potential. Minimalism serves as a tool to attain freedom, breaking free from fear, worry, overwhelm, guilt, and depression, liberating you from the consumer culture's trappings. In essence, minimalism helps you focus on what truly matters, leading to happiness, fulfilment, and ultimate freedom.

Marie Kondo, the author of "Life-Changing Magic of Tidying Up," is often recognized as a minimalist. However, her post on her website, KonMari Method™, announces that "KonMari Is Not Minimalism," her method of "tidying up" is translated into "living with less" and "living with items you truly cherish." She equates Joy as a personal experience, and both minimalism and the KonMari Method™ embrace this. Your ideal life and space are unique, so if minimalism brings you joy, that's great. Similarly, if you find joy in having many items, that's okay too. The KonMari Method™ emphasises living with things that truly bring you happiness. This method is linked to minimalism because it often reveals that people have been keeping items they no longer love or never truly cherished. No matter what, both ways advocate for decluttering your life of needless things. One calls it tidying up, and another minimalism. What is noticeable is that both ask you to keep your sights on getting rid of bestrews and keep things that give you happiness and joy. Both promise their audiences an exciting journey of life; in a journey, you discover your true nature and pure potential; that is what you are, the real you.

The ideal aim of human beings is to gain both intellectual as well as emotional maturity. While society has us focused more on intellectualism,   emotional maturity can elevate us to a higher level of consciousness, sparking significant changes in our lives. This shift is marked by a transformation where you barely resemble your former self. You become motivated to change, experience intense focus, crave a more meaningful life, and discover your higher purpose. If your mind is cluttered with unnecessary thoughts and distractions, a shift in consciousness becomes essential to declutter your mental space.

Decluttering is problematic because it represents the value you bought. It requires you to be a deep thinker. It is challenging even if we've decided to part with some of the stuff.

....

In Erica Buist's article "Do Something Brainy - Why Tidying Up Can Change Your Life," she highlights the clutter in our homes as a reflection of cluttered minds. The minimalist approach advocated by Joshua Fields Millburn and Ryan Nicodemus, known as "The Minimalists," involves shedding unnecessary possessions and simplifying life. Nicodemus's transformation from a hectic, possession-driven lifestyle to deliberate time management demonstrates the benefits of decluttering, leading to a more fulfilling and compassionate existence. By decluttering both our physical spaces and minds, we can truly savour life's richness.

Critical thinking can give us a great life is what we need, and if minimalism can give us that high, why not change your lifestyle and enjoy the fun? Indeed, clutter can be a mental drain, as Leon Ho, Founder, and CEO of Life Hacks, points out. Ignoring the chaos in your surroundings, whether it's noise or distractions, consumes valuable mental energy, leaving your brain passive and unable to focus effectively. Decluttering, minimising, or tidying up helps you clean your house and relaxes your mind. Another fantastic outcome of decluttering is that you join the United Nations Sustainable Development Goals, a "Global Goal for Climate Action" that, too, from the comfort of your home. The United Nations preamble, beginning with the "We the People of United Nations Determined", is a brief introductory statement of the Constitution's fundamental purpose and guiding principles. It promises Peace, Dignity, and Equality on a Healthy Planet. By decluttering, you will be doing excellent service because it means "consuming less" and consuming fewer addresses global warming. The easiest way to reduce greenhouse gas emissions is to consume less or buy less. People usually are resigned to thinking that climate control is too big an issue to engage in. They believe the responsibility lies with the Governments of the earth simply because they are unaware of their powers and blindly believe what they are being told. That is the direct impact that minimalism contains.

We feel helpless and do not exercise our power simply because the invisible hands of market forces and self-preserving plans of governments have so conditioned our minds that we no longer resort to our limitless critical thinking capacity. One good way to retrieve your critical mind is to become a part of minimalism, a mission more appropriate for the present because it helps change the climate. Forget not that you, the consumers, have been driving the economy. On the whims of marketing people, Consumers are making the GDP, and the stock market swings between bull and bear, unrealistically when they are not applying their analytical minds. Minimalism allows you to think profoundly and regulate your powers for your health and the good of the earth and humanity. Are you ready to join the crusade? You need to. It is revolutionary and meaningful. After all, life has no charm if it has no meaning. Wear a glass of your inner vision through which you can see reality. This glass will let you know the truth that enables you to see the colour of your spirit that was not perceptible to you through a conditioned mind. And to make it more amusing, you need a purpose, and the purpose is nothing but to be a part of climate activists by reducing your carbon footprint to control global warming - a threat to the existence of humanity. While reducing your footprint, you not only reduce global warming, but you also become a critical thinker.

TECHNOCRACY

Mother Nature has reset - repaired, and healed - itself for millions of years whenever it ran down. But this time, a handful of her distraught children have caused so much maltreatment and destruction to Earth -   Mother Earth - that it cannot reset itself without our help. It needs urgent help from us to avert severe global warming and climate change to save humanity from being ruined. The climate has already warmed up to a dangerous level. If the change is not slowed down, we will see large-scale hazards to human health. The Paris Agreement, now at 5 years, sees leaders talking about far-off goals and tricky "net zero" plans. Greta Thunberg tweets about this, but she believes that our true hope lies in the people.

You see, there's a growing concern about a powerful technocracy that's taking away our ability to make decisions and control our destiny. They're threatening what we call "human agency," which is the power we have to choose and make meaningful changes in our lives. This power only works when we think for ourselves and pick the best influences around us. So, my dear, let's remember that hope isn't just in promises from leaders but in the strength of the people.

In Jillianne Code's article on "Agency for Learning," she discusses intention, motivation, self-efficacy, and self-regulation, all crucial for our ability to learn and grow. Now, turning to Adam

Hall's article about the challenge to state sovereignty due to the promotion of human rights, he mentions that universal human rights can clash with the traditional definition of sovereignty, which grants states non-intervention in their internal affairs.

However, it's the technocrats who pose a real threat. They speak of the "Technotronic Era," where society becomes more controlled and directed. An elite group claims power through scientific knowledge and uses modern techniques to influence public behaviour and keep a close watch on us. Patric M. Wood, in his book "Technocracy is Rising: The Trojan Horse of Global Transformation," warns that this "New World Order" isn't about communalism, socialism, or fascism; it's about technocracy. He mentions global programs like Agenda 21, Sustainable Development, and others and believes the logical outcome of technocracy is a scientific dictatorship. So, let's stay vigilant and protect our agency and sovereignty.

Technocracy is not a rule of the people, for the people, and by the people, but a decree; like the Greek god Hermes, they are gods of eloquence, good fortune, and trade as well as of cunning, fraud, and theft.

In a recent interview, Wood, an expert on technocracy, explained that technocrats define technocracy as the scientific management of society to provide goods and services to the entire population.

Wood also mentioned prominent figures like Bill Gates, Elon Musk, Eric Schmidt, and Jeff Bezos, labelling them as technocrats. He emphasised that they don't align with fascism, socialism, or communism but prioritise their own agendas over individual human life. On a similar note, Douglas Kruger, a renowned author and Mensa member, expressed concerns in an interview about the Great Reset plan by the WEF and UNO. He pointed out that despite claims of collective ownership, those in power would be the true owners. Powerful individuals in finance, banking, and business, along with government leaders, aim to rebuild economies after covert lockdowns. However, Kruger cautioned against this collectivist approach, emphasising the importance of personal ownership. He highlighted the phrase "You will own nothing, and you will be happy" as a concerning aspect of their proposal.

I recommend reading the article "Who Wants to Be a Slave? The Convergence of Human Data" by Danial Broudy and Makoto Arakaki from Okinawa Christian University in Japan. They delve into how digital tools pose a threat to human agency and sovereignty. They mention Marshall McLuhan's observation from the 1960s that humans are tool makers whose tools eventually reshape them. Today, in the Information Age, the internet serves as the global nervous system for humankind, and this article explores how media manipulate public opinion about and consent for new digital tools and techniques that threaten human agency and sovereignty. The threat has intensified in the current pandemic milieu. It's essential to understand this within the context of historical attempts to control populations through sophisticated computing tools. Eric Schmidt, responding to criticism about Google's data practices, suggested that if you want privacy, maybe you shouldn't do things you want to hide. This implies that tech companies and their tools have become agents of state authority.

Computers process data. Data is a type of energy; whether it be sophisticated machines like an automobile, aeroplane, rocket or supercomputer, everything is made up with the help of software. The software sends an instruction to the computer hardware. The hardware processes the data or, in other words, energy. Without managing data or energy, technological advances would not have been possible - manipulating atomic, subatomic, quanta and even conscious energy. Both electromagnetic fields and consciousness are considered forms of material reality. In simpler terms, consciousness can be viewed as a type of energy, akin to kinetic or electrical energy. What's crucial to note is that our consciousness can be influenced and controlled without us realising the extent of it. Our thoughts, ideas, and imaginations are energies masterfully manipulated and controlled by marketers. In more straightforward way, people tend to call it "brainwashing". Brainwashing is nothing but manipulating consciousness. Marketers use beautiful words – advertisements – to brainwash people, and brainwashed people accept and believe whatever the marketers offer without finding their truthfulness.

With the suppression of dissenting voices since 9/11, genuine political discourse has been overshadowed by corporate mythologies and algorithms. They condition us to believe that the technocracy-led neoliberal global order isn't just beneficial but essential. The message is clear: resisting social change imposed by these tools is futile.

If the technocrats have their way, we will no longer be free to determine our own future and progress. Technocrats have long back planned to reset the human population and economy by depopulating the world population and controlling the economy artificially against the laws of nature. COVID-19 has allowed them to quicken their plan. Through the facade of UNO and WEF, they have planned to artificially reset the human population and economy to bring in The New World Order. Over 50,000 physicians and health scientists endorsed the Barrington Declaration (Oct 4, 2020) opposing lockdowns. The website gbdeclaration.org now boasts over 933,700 signatories. Technocrats, working closely with global government leaders, are aggressively pushing for mass vaccination. They've set up facilities to produce 100-150 million prefilled syringes to administer vaccines to billions within a year. They plan to rule all governments worldwide.

Some believe the New World Order aims for a one-world government to exert control over people. It's no longer considered a conspiracy theory by many; it's seen as a real concern. These people have already destroyed the economy by conditioning people's minds. People are already poor and illiterate as they do not have their own thoughts and imagination. They think not nothing else except what the technocrats want them to think. With their mega plan to vaccinate every individual on the planet, they will control humankind even more masterly as people are vaccinated. Their data are stored in supercomputers and cluster computers controlled by technocrats. There will be no privacy. And with the help of artificial intelligence, they will make people out of jobs.

Literacy is squandered if people do not engage in the essential practice of unlearning and relearning, leaving them in a state of impoverished thinking. Unlearning means doubting everything you have learned. People never doubted the gods of the words - technocrats and oligarchy - and pulled the economy to the point of destruction of people and destruction of the climate. We have come to this pass simply because, for decades, we have supported them without doubting their sham words, helping them turn their obnoxious plan into reality. What really happened was that they took great undue advantage of the innocent and ignorant people of the earth. They made the whole world sick physically, mentally, and emotionally. They made people feel sad, miserable, gloomy, unlucky, and unhappy. People were unhappy and wanted to know the mantra for happiness. And the mantra these technocrats and oligarchy offered was that only possessions could make them happy, for which they had to work hard and make lots of money. They dangled attractive carrots before them, which made people mad. People drove the economy faster, making them sick and sicker and often sent them into traumatic experiences, physical, mental and psychological.

We have come to this grim pass because we accepted their offering, blindfolded, never doubting their despicable intentions, though unknowingly. But dazzled by the ornate words of technocrats, we fell prey to it. We didn't know the reality nor tried to probe into its nitty-gritty; we didn't see the truth that we are born with an all-powerful, all-knowing cosmic mind with the complete knowledge of what is true and what is untrue, what is right and what is wrong, what is wise what is unwise. Nevertheless, we, the people of the world, still have the power to right the wrongs done by us. And the way is that we must realise our mistakes; we must recognize that we are not ordinary animals. We are unusual animals. We are unique and conscious animals with the immense power to manage our own evolution. We need to become more deliberate and stand up to take our freedom back by "Pushing the Envelope for Being Human." Be truthful to yourself and your cosmic mind and remember, Truth wins in the end.

CHAPTER FOURTEEN

CARBON FOOTPRINT

It's eye-opening to discover that Bill Gates alone produced a staggering 1600 tons of carbon dioxide in 2017 just from his flights, as reported by Ben Webster in "Jet-setting stars exposed over hypocrisy on climate change." These super-rich individuals, including Gates, are responsible for a disproportionately high amount of carbon pollution compared to the poorest half of humanity, according to Oxfam. It's essential to recognize that global challenges, like climate change, affect us all. Among the barrage of coronavirus news, there has been much good news.

Natasha Daly's article in National Geographic, titled "Fake animal news abounds on social media as coronavirus upends life," sheds light on the spread of misleading stories about wildlife during the pandemic. These stories, often shared on platforms like Twitter, Instagram, and TikTok, depicted animals thriving in the absence of human activity. However, as Daly clarifies, many of these reports were not accurate. Despite knowing the misinformation, some individuals, like Kaveri Ganga Pathy Ahuja, chose not to delete their viral tweets, arguing that the positive impact on the environment was still relevant. Reduced activities are what matters and have given great relief to climate activists. We know that mindless aggressive activities of humans cause climate change; because of this behaviour, people lose their capacity to reason. As the US withdrew from the Paris Agreement, it seemed almost impossible to contain climate change. Climate change is no less than a miracle in these few months. The invisible hands have become indeed invisible to the great relief, perhaps, every rational person who was pained to see the harm done to Mother Nature. Of course, the toll could be very high, but It may save humanity from going extinct, which is more than welcome.

Maxine Harley, in her article titled "The Real Problem Is A Lack Of Connection," highlights the impact of a fast-paced and emotionally disconnected society. She emphasises that people are driven to share posts that evoke emotions, seeking a deeper connection with themselves and others. In this society, there's often a sense of emptiness, leaving individuals unsure of their identities, desires, and how to achieve them. Harley suggests that to overcome this feeling of "existential despair," people can reconnect with essential aspects of life such as awareness, love, inner peace, comfort, safety, and the present moment.   Another way out is to reduce your carbon footprint, which will require you to be a critical thinker of your actions - thought action or otherwise.

As I mentioned in previous chapters,   by the time one disposes of a potato chip 167g packet priced at 10 cents, it has produced 75g of carbon footprint (potato cooked at home produces only 2.9g CO_2). One has the choice to reduce that carbon footprint, which may not be enough but it is a starting point. Jeffrey Moyer, the chair of the National Organic Standards Board, speaks candidly about the concerns within the potato industry: "I've talked with potato growers who say point-blank they would never eat the potatoes they sell. They have separate plots where they grow potatoes for themselves without all the chemicals." This quote underscores the reservations some growers have about the use of chemicals in commercial potato production. Every farm product has grown inorganically, and machine-processed food causes enormous carbon costs and is unsuitable for your health. Thanks to the farm-to-table movement, more people are becoming aware of it. Slowly but surely, people are buying fresh organic vegetables from farmer's markets or growing their own vegetables, herbs, and fruits in their own kitchen gardens. A lot of people grow vegetables on their terraces by applying hydroponic and/or grow-bag systems.

The selling of unhealthy processed foods is no less than a crime. It is unethical. Even though there are ethical lessons taught in business schools, businesses bypass government laws to make 'dough'. The invisible hands of market forces and the never-ending greed of the super-rich ensure that their pockets remain full, allowing them to exploit the earth's resources and the resources of the ignorant people. The pursuit of wealth at any cost has taken a toll on the world, affecting physical, mental, and emotional well-being. It's disheartening to witness how greed can lead people to disregard Mother Nature, their fellow human beings, and even themselves. I have witnessed how society has changed. It wasn't this prominent when I was young. People still had ethics in business. The article emphasises our interconnectedness with Mother Nature, reminding us that we are all her children. Furthermore, the longest-running bull market in history, which began in 2009, has contributed to a growing wealth gap between the rich and the poor, highlighting the consequences of unchecked greed.

The COVID-19 pandemic, with its global impact, raises questions about its origins and the potential for positive change. Some believe it could ultimately lead to positive outcomes, such as reducing wealth inequality and addressing environmental issues like climate change. It's crucial to reflect on our relationship with nature and our responsibility towards one another and the planet. It is believed that coronavirus will change the world for the better. Epidemiologists are still grappling with the severity of the coronavirus pandemic, while pundits confidently predict that it will bring lasting change. There are various opinions, with some suggesting it will transform globalisation for the better and even potentially impact populism. However, it's essential to consider that every human activity generates CO2, and maintaining a balance is crucial. When we emit more CO2 than our environment can absorb, it leads to problems.

The average carbon footprint of an American produces 16 tons a year. Globally, the average carbon footprint is closer to 4 tons. It should be less than 2 tons. If any individual's carbon footprint is more than 2 tons, they need to reduce it. The website "The Nature Conservancy" has a Carbon Footprint Calculator to help you with this.   If you are producing a carbon footprint of more than what you are supposed to produce, you are polluting the environment to the detriment of your own health and the health of Mother Earth and its children. Nature operates without waste; everything has a purpose and is reused. Fallen leaves, for example, become mulch to nourish trees. Animals in nature only take what they need to survive. The concept of wastefulness, as we know it, is a human-made problem, resulting from our consumption patterns, causing harm to the environment. Yes, we are the cause for producing garbage considerably more than nature can absorb due to our overconsumption pattern. As we have been the cause of the folly, we need to own up to the responsibility, reduce our overconsumption habits and reduce our carbon footprint.

When you embrace self-care practices and nurture yourself, you become better equipped to care for and love others. Just as all organisms share the purpose of survival, humans, as multicellular organisms, have the same core objective. Survival for all organisms relies on the interconnected food chain and food web, where producers like plants create their own food through photosynthesis, and consumers like animals obtain energy by consuming other organisms. In the event of a break in the food chain, it can lead to ecosystem imbalances or even a collapse, with global warming and climate change posing a significant threat. Extreme weather conditions resulting from these changes can disrupt food security and, ultimately, lead to conflicts when people suffer from hunger and desperation. The causes of climate change include actions like burning fossil fuels, deforestation, and livestock farming, which release significant amounts of greenhouse gases into the atmosphere, intensifying the greenhouse effect and leading to global warming. Humans are primarily responsible for this, as human activities have significantly increased the concentration of these heat-trapping gases in the atmosphere. This increase in greenhouse gases, including carbon dioxide, methane, nitrous oxide, ozone, and various chlorofluorocarbons, has been identified by climate scientists as the primary driver behind the 1.8°F (1.0°C) increase in global average temperature since the late nineteenth century. And how human activity emits heat! Heat is emitted when we consume energy. That is not a problem. When there is life, there is activity, and energy is consumed when there is activity.

The problem arises when we consume indirect energy more than we should consume. Indirect energy consumption refers to the energy used in the production of various items, such as vehicles, machinery, appliances, buildings, and infrastructure within the food system. It also includes maintaining a supply of spare parts and equipment for repairs. The real issue lies in the overconsumption of indirect energy, a problem many are unaware of.

However, only reducing CO2 doesn't serve the greater purpose: to heal yourself and the world. It would be a welcome gesture if you could make more people aware of it.

....

Yes, Earth's climate has naturally fluctuated throughout history, with ice ages and warm periods occurring in roughly 100,000-year cycles. However, in the last century, the planet's average surface temperature has risen by approximately 1.0°F, with the warmest years occurring since 1980. This warming trend is confirmed by NASA scientists, who have observed significant temperature increases in recent decades. Despite natural climate variations, 97 per cent of working climate scientists agree that the current warming is primarily driven by human activities, such as the increase in greenhouse gas emissions. CO2 levels have risen significantly since the Industrial Revolution, reaching over 400 ppm in 2015 and continuing to climb.

Every living entity requires energy to fuel its growth, reproduction, structural maintenance, and responses to its surroundings. Metabolism represents the collection of vital chemical processes that enable organisms to convert the stored chemical energy within molecules into usable energy for cellular functions. Plants harness the energy from sunlight to create the nutrients they require, while other organisms, known as heterotrophs, consume either plants or animals to obtain energy and nutrients. This interconnected web of energy transfer is termed the food supply chain or food system, and problems arise when disruptions occur within this system.

The food supply chain is a complex yet vital food production mechanism that is indispensable for global sustainability and food security. Preserving the integrity of this chain is crucial for the survival of all organisms, including us. Regrettably, many of us tend to take our food supply for granted, overlooking the fact that even a single disruption in this chain can result in shortages, contamination, or higher prices.

Excessive energy production and consumption are the root causes of global warming. This issue has intensified since the industrial and digital revolutions. People globally embraced industry offerings without critical thinking, driven by ignorance. Philosophers like Plato and Descartes supported the idea of innate human knowledge.

Deepak Chopra's "The Seven Spiritual Laws of Success" introduces the Law of Pure Potentiality, highlighting our inherent pure consciousness as a source of limitless creativity. Unfortunately, our ignorance hinders us from tapping into this potential. This boundless potential is accessible to everyone but often goes unnoticed due to our ignorance. We missed opportunities because those who understood it couldn't convey it. We were captivated by marketers' narratives, preventing us from discovering our true selves. Embracing self-referral, guided by inner spirit, is the key, unlike object-referral, which lets external factors shape our reality. Deepak Chopra offers these profound insights.

When you arrive at the core of your being, your genuine nature, you know who you really are. Unaware you have been connecting with your genuine self very often. Now you can experience it with full awareness. In this state of awareness, you can connect with your true self. You only need to intend to with your full awareness and attention consciously. What you need is little time to spend in solitude. This is your genuine nature. Then, you will see clearly that there is no difference between you and other human beings. This is your true nature - the real you. That is the reality of the 750 billion people on the planet Earth we are citizens of; seen from here, we are all one; every single person has the same purpose - to serve humanity - a baby knows this. It sees no difference from one to another. The source of all its actions is its true self - the seat of truth.

METAHUMAN

In DC Comics' DC Universe, metahumans are humans with superpowers, like Batman, Superman, and Wonder Woman. Deepak Chopra's book, "Metahuman: Unleashing Your Infinite Potentiality," suggests that all humans have untapped potential to develop superpowers within themselves. The book's final section provides 31 days of lessons for those interested in becoming metahumans. Annabel Gutterman, a Time journalist, questions if 31 days are enough for this transformation, to which Deepak Chopra responds that it's an experiment, and curiosity is a powerful teacher. In the interview titled "Deepak Chopra Wants You to Have More Meaningful Life," Chopra explains how we can transcend human constructs to connect with our true selves. He emphasises that while human constructs like money, geography, and nation-states are necessary, they should not limit our experience of life. Going beyond these constructs allows us to find more meaning in life, guided by a higher perspective of the self.

Your true self has the power to view things from a higher perspective. Unfortunately, most of the human population is ignorant of the power of their innate abilities, the abilities of their true self, from where you can watch your higher perspective and finding solutions to all problems becomes unchallenging. We cannot find it because of our ignorance of the powers of our true selves. When your ignorance is removed, life becomes exciting. I believe that his podcast is trying to remove ignorance and help you become a metahuman. Removing ignorance from your life can make it more exciting. Deepak Chopra's podcast aims to eliminate ignorance and help you become a metahuman. In another article authored by Chopra, he explains that when people face challenges or goals, they often feel the need to take immediate action. However, he suggests that every human problem is rooted in consciousness, which is also where the solutions can be found. Becoming a metahuman means delving into the root of both problems and solutions.

"Vasudhaiva Kutumbakam" is a Sanskrit phrase from Hindu texts, including the Maha Upanishad, which translates to "The World Is One Family." This phrase conveys the idea that all living beings on Earth are part of a single family, with "Vasudha" meaning "Earth" and "Kutumbakam" meaning "Family." The COVID-19 pandemic has served as a reminder of the truth behind this ancient concept. This virus, like all of nature, does not discriminate based on man-made distinctions; it does not respect the rich, and powerful any more than the poor and powerless – even prime ministers and princes have suffered its affliction, and a princess of Spain has died. It does not bother with whether a person is Hindu or Muslim, Indian or Pakistani, high caste or low, black or Asian or white. It only recognizes the human family, the species," writes Samarat in his article, "Coronavirus has shaken our standing in the world. Can it spark fundamental thinking of priorities?". The coronavirus's impact on the global economy, as discussed by Larry Elliott in his article "Blindsided: how coronavirus felled the global economy in 100 days," has economists and society pondering whether there's a need to return to the same pre-pandemic economic norms. Some are relieved by the temporary respite it has given to nature. People have been appreciating the beauty of blossoms and nature's resurgence during the lockdown, as highlighted by Peter C. Baker and Steven Morris in their articles. This moment prompts us to question whether we should aim to go back to the previous state of affairs, which had its share of problems, or if we should consider new approaches for a better future. Distrust is the root cause of chaos in the world. Public trust is rapidly declining worldwide, affecting how we relate to each other, our governments, and various institutions. This distrust is evident in social media, politics, communities, and even our daily interactions. It hampers public discourse and cooperation, hindering progress.

The collective erosion of trust undermines the ability of institutions to serve their intended purpose. Rebuilding trust is challenging, and if not addressed, its consequences may persist for years to come. Written by Kristin M. Lord, CEO of IREX, an organisation committed to creating a more just, prosperous, and inclusive world by empowering youth, fostering leadership, strengthening institutions, and providing access to quality education and information.

One of the best ways to bring back trust among people is that the way to get back is for as many people to be made metahuman as possible. Absolutely, there's no project more valuable than discovering your authentic self.

This book, too, is an attempt to enable you to discover the metahuman in you; it is simple. You only need to watch your awareness levels and upgrade them from "contracted to pure awareness." The purpose of this book is to guide you on how to search to upgrade your awareness level to enlighten you.

VAULTING AMBITIONS

Much like Victor Frankenstein's creation, the super-rich have birthed a global economic monster. Their relentless pursuit of wealth infects people worldwide, driving them toward quick riches and fueling senseless competition. This obsession extends to all aspects of life, leaving no room for values beyond money. It infiltrates homes, schools, and organisations, benefiting the wealthy while neglecting ethical values.

Similar to Victor Frankenstein's ambition leading to his downfall, the super-rich have created an economy that now dominates the world. Their relentless pursuit of wealth has infected people globally, fostering a culture of cutthroat competition where everyone strives for rapid riches, losing sight of ethical values and true happiness. People have lost their individuality. The whole world is confused, and the cause of confusion is that they haven't yet found the values of life. They don't know that for a human not to "be humane" is no less than a curse.

The world sadly lacks humanity, even among its influential figures—the super-rich who govern it. Ensnared by wealth's allure, they display inhumane behaviour, causing nearly irreversible global damage. They must acknowledge their responsibility for world suffering and act promptly to save themselves, Mother Earth, and humanity. Climate change warnings remind them to empathise with Earth and its underprivileged inhabitants, as they share the same mother, Mother Nature. How can they remain indifferent to their kin and relatives? How can they ignore Mother Nature's suffering, who lovingly nurtured them? She sustains them every second, despite their faults. Their ego is their enemy, creating vast inequality and crises. They must realise that money can't ensure survival, just as vast fortunes can vanish in disasters and wars. According to Forbes magazine, the damages from the Ukraine war amount to $108 billion.

"Vishwaguru" is a term that conveys the idea of a teacher or master of the entire world, a preceptor for humanity. However, the super-rich, who were often regarded as Vishwagurus, have seemingly betrayed this noble title. Rather than leading humanity towards peace and harmony, they have contributed to global problems through their exploitation of both the planet and its inhabitants. History has seen many civilizations collapse, but all were local or regional, but today's failures have inundated the entire world. If emergency measures are not initiated with great immediacy, it will be almost impossible to reverse climate change. Sadly, most of the world population is ignorant and doesn't know that they, unwittingly, have been participants of the super rich's plan by driving the economic chariot at a dizzying speed through their habit of overconsumption.   In this uncertainty, the super-rich have power, and if they galvanise themselves together, they can take emergency measures to save humanity from going extinct. They should be Vishwaguru in the true sense. If they introspect, they will find that they have always been motivated by their childish thoughts. They should realise and become sober.

As a child, the natural inclination is to want to possess and control beautiful things, believing that it leads to love and happiness. However, this desire for control and possessions stems from the ego, and true mastery involves transcending the ego. The guru's role is to help individuals let go of their ego and realise their true selves, and this inner transformation is not something that can be bought with money. Instead, the super-rich should strive to become Vishwaguru, using their power to change the world for the better and save the planet from hardship.

The evolution of human intelligence is closely linked to the development of the human brain. Sticking to a fixed belief system can hinder the evolution of intelligence. Curiosity thrives when challenging common beliefs. The super-rich, who have clung to the belief in the "invisible hand" and self-interest, limit their intellectual potential. The human mind is a remarkable masterpiece with immense potential.

However, most of the potential remains unused to most people since it is not us who are in charge of things; our Minds take control of us. Our Minds are rushing through life with us like a car running without a driver, causing us constant suffering and sorrow. But if we were able to control our minds, our lives would change completely. The mad rush of our lives could transform into a beautiful, creative dance that brings happiness instead of pain. This transformation is discussed in an article titled "The Human Mind is a Wonderful Masterpiece, but Can also be a Dangerous Master." The super-rich, due to their rigid beliefs, haven't mastered their minds, but Brian Thompson's "Words of Wisdom" can help them challenge their unexamined beliefs and find freedom in self-awareness.

Connecting with joy is essential, as Earth was meant for joy, according to Alice Walker. Joy is the Universe's balanced source, impacting the evolution of the self, our bodies, and life's purpose. However, the super-rich seem to have lost this connection, leading to a conflicted and fragmented world. Ulhas Pagey's article "The World is One Family" emphasises the need for the super-rich to reconnect with the world as members of one family and become true Vishwagurus, using their power responsibly.

The goal of life is to achieve peace of mind, but disconnection has made it elusive. The need of the hour is that the super-rich and every citizen of the globe must realise that this disconnection has caused a significant imbalance, and they all must try their best to reestablish the lost connection to bring back peace in the world.

....

To be a Vishwaguru (teacher/master of the world) is not easy, but we must strive at least to be a guru (a reformer). A reformer reforms the society of the times in all its aspects. Ralph Waldo Emerson, in his lecture "Man the Reformer," posed the question, "What is a man born for but to be a Reformer?" He saw humanity's purpose as reformers, remaking what others have created, renouncing falsehoods, and restoring truth and goodness. Emerson compared this to the continuous renewal of nature, where each day brings a new opportunity and every heartbeat offers a fresh start.

To reform, the human body is in the DNA of every human cell. They work hard to increase their chance of survival. These cells are no less than humans. Look at your 30/40 trillion cells. Their job is to reform the colony of the body they occupy. They keep improving and repairing our bodies, working ceaselessly without stopping or pausing even for a nanosecond to heal them and protect us from outside invaders such as bacteria, viruses, fungi, and toxins and keep our beings - bodies - in perfect order. They are free from judgement and/or ideologies and work hard together single-mindedly with one purpose – to keep the body free from all-body disorders. Humans, like these dedicated practitioners, are born with an innate instinct for reform, but we often forget it due to the influence of our ego-driven minds and rigid belief systems. This forgetting leaves an emptiness in us, depleting our energy and leading to emotional exhaustion. This void is the neglected reformer within, yearning to break free from the self-imposed prison of ego and reconnect with the global family. To rediscover this inner reformer, we can draw inspiration from our carefree childhood or the passionate young activists like Greta Thunberg, who are striving to reform the world and challenge the recklessness of the super-rich and governments. Greta's "Friday for Future" movement, which mobilised millions of students globally, serves as a powerful example of this awakening.

My dear, In the pursuit of true leadership, often described as a Vishwaguru, one must understand the profound connection between self-actualization and the betterment of our world. A Vishwaguru is a beacon of knowledge, both internal and external, guiding humanity towards a harmonious existence. Their passion and drive stem from their innate connection to their reformer selves, a quality inherent in every human being. Just as our body's cells continually work to reform and heal our physical selves, we, as humans, are born with the responsibility to reform our beloved planet, Mother Earth. It's a duty ingrained within us. Much like our bodies cannot thrive without constant self-improvement at the cellular level, Mother Nature too is suffering due to our negligence. Unintentionally, we have pushed Mother Nature to the brink of peril, endangering not only our own lives but the survival of our entire human family.

In this critical juncture, our only recourse is to awaken the reformer within us and actively engage in reshaping the ideologies that have divided our world. The true reformer's mission is to mend the wounds of Mother Earth and her children. However, we cannot hope to reform the world without first reforming and healing ourselves.

The question then becomes, how do we embark on this journey of self-reform? The answers lie in the chapters that follow, where we shall explore the path towards healing and transformation.

LOVE THYSELF

The universe, my dear, emerged with the Big Bang, birthing evolution simultaneously. Before that explosion, there was nothing; everything began then. Every celestial body - the suns, moons, stars, galaxies, and planets, even our own Earth, and all that dwells upon it, are threads woven into the vast tapestry of the universe. Life, including us humans, is a result of this cosmic journey spanning billions of years. We evolved over time, building upon the legacy of our predecessors, and gradually becoming the unique beings we are. Yet, a problem arose when some humans believed in their superiority over other life forms.

This perception has brought discord. We must return to a harmonious understanding of our place within this interconnected web of existence. In reality, this belief is based on ignorance, as science shows that animals can possess cognitive abilities superior to humans. This sense of superiority leads to a desire for domination and blinds us to the truth that we are not more intelligent or superior; we are simply part of the ongoing process of evolution. No other organism except the human organism can speak a complex language and use logic and intellect to reason. Otherwise, there is no difference between the human organism and other organisms. You automatically follow universal laws like all other organisms when you have no logical mind. Your self-awareness that you are a being that can think logically and that other living beings cannot make you smug. You are complacent because you think you are holier-than-thou; you think so because you are ignorant of reality.

It's commendable that you possess a cognitive mind, which encompasses the process of gaining knowledge and understanding through thoughts, experiences, and senses. Undoubtedly, you have intelligence and the potential to acquire knowledge. However, as a parent, I find it regrettable that you may not be fully harnessing your cognitive abilities. This will eventually make you emotionally dependent. People are dependent because they do not utilise their minds to acquire knowledge about the realities of their lives. All organisms have life; all organisms have a body, mind, consciousness and soul; the human organism, too, has a body, mind consciousness and soul. The distinction lies not in the physical aspect but in the realm of the mind. While animals and humans share many cognitive components, there exists a significant cognitive divide. Humans possess a unique level of self-awareness, being conscious of their consciousness, setting them apart from other organisms. Indeed, we humans are conscious and intelligent. What is regrettable is that though conscious and intelligent, we are not entirely conscious. We don't know the reality of our being. We are ignorant of the truth about ourselves. We do not know who we are, what our bodies are made of or how they function. We know nothing about our minds and souls. When you are not aware of yourself, you are confused. When you are confused, there is chaos everywhere within or without.

Increasing self-knowledge – knowledge about your body, mind and soul – is the solution. And the way is self-love. It was self-love that kept the universe glued together since its inception. Except for the human organism, all organisms are held together because of self-love. Self-love in animals is innate. But because of intelligence humans need to love themselves consciously.

Loving yourself means knowing your body, mind and soul. Loving oneself begins with knowing oneself. You possess the intelligence to explore any knowledge you desire. However, it's disheartening to see that your intelligence may not always be used wisely. Remaining unaware of your complete self is akin to ignorance, my dear, and it's essential to acknowledge this. How can one truly love oneself without grasping the essence of their body, mind, and soul? I understand that at times, you may have hesitated to embrace reality, thinking it beyond human capacity. But please understand, my dear, that the pursuit of knowledge, especially self-knowledge, is an act of self-love. It's a journey of discovery that can bring profound joy and fulfilment.   Thanks to breakthroughs in science and panpsychism, we know the reality of life; we know almost everything. Won't it be imprudent if we don't try to know the truth? And a simple way to know yourself is to love yourself.

....

Many scientists, including Stephen Hawking, posit that there was nothing before the Big Bang. According to Hawking, this theory hinges on the idea that the universe lacks boundaries. He emphasised this during a conversation with physicist Neil deGrasse Tyson on the 'Star Talk' show broadcasted on the National Geographic Channel.

I take the liberty to conjecture; an educated guess. If there was nothing, there was the energy of consciousness—the conscious energy of the Cosmic Mother. Cosmic Mother's consciousness conceived the idea of creating a universe. She loved the idea intensely. Her intense longing made her meditate with firm intention and undivided passionate attention and love. She meditated/incubated for millions and millions and millions of years and delivered a magnificent universe with a Big Bang when it matured. Love was the Cosmic Mother's inspiration. That Cosmic Mother's love keeps the universe glued together. The universe and every part of the universe are Cosmic Mother's Love children – a family that has grown large. Every part of the universal space is occupied with the soul of that cosmic love; that love (gravity) holds the universe together. The soul of every life on earth is love. All organisms are filled with love. The human organism is no different; humans, too, are filled with compassionate love. But we miss it because we are excessively engaged with our self-ego. We are not aware of this enemy hidden inside of us. It is a matter of recognising it and increasing our awareness about it; once we become aware of that hidden enemy, it won't be hard to get rid of our ego. And the best way to get rid of your ego is to develop a positive attitude towards life and the best way to have a positive attitude is to "love thyself".

The ancient Greek saying "Know Thyself" could be reframed as "Love Thyself," which I find more meaningful. Self-love and self-understanding are intertwined; as you understand yourself better, your love for yourself deepens, and so does respect. This concept aligns with Thich Nhat Hanh's idea that love and understanding are interconnected. Self-love and self-care are like a specialist doctor diagnosing and treating you accurately – the first step towards effective care. The journey of self-knowledge is endless, as described by J. Krishnamurti, offering ongoing clarity and insight into oneself. Not knowing or not loving yourself is the cause of all your troubles. Finding yourself means knowing who you are, where you have come from, what your body is made of, and how your body, mind and soul function. Finding yourself means you are evolving and growing to your full potential. Knowing your full potential means beginning to end your problems.   And the best way to find your full potential is to Love Thyself.

In Chandresh Bhardwaj's book "Break the Norm: Question Everything You Think You Know About God and Truth, Life and Death, Love and Sex," he offers a powerful approach to self-discovery and realising one's divine potential, as acknowledged by Deepak Chopra. To be a catalyst for change and a critical thinker, you must break the norms and embrace self-love, as emphasised by Janine Ripper and Leo Tolstoy's wisdom. Chinny Okoye's advice in The Guardian reinforces the importance of resilience, consistency, self-love, and personal transformation in effecting change. Minimalism serves as a pathway to enhance critical thinking and fosters a missionary spirit that promotes compassion for oneself and others. According to Sandi Schwartz, compassion is an innate human instinct that contributes to happiness and the desire to alleviate others' suffering, leading to what she calls the "helper's high." You, too, must have felt the "helpers high" on people who were needy and wanting to help; I remember you being good to the poor during your childhood. But we become indifferent when we grow up because of parents' ignorance who couldn't nurture empathy in their children. While compassion is innate, nurturing it is crucial, as Erin Lanahan suggests in her article "5 Ways to Feel More Love and Compassion for Yourself and Others." Turning inward and seeking guidance from your higher wisdom can reveal areas where you may lack qualities like love, trust, compassion, forgiveness, and acceptance. A minimalist perspective encourages compassion not only for yourself but also for others on the shared journey of life. Remember,   every action has consequences, both for your well-being and that of your fellow travellers, underscores the importance of considerate actions.

Self-love, fundamentally, is an act of survival, empowering care for others. Like all life, we share this innate drive. Survival depends on the intricate web of life, from plant producers to animal consumers. Yet, human actions like burning fossil fuels, deforestation, and intensive farming have raised temperatures. Our activities emit heat, and overconsumption of indirect energy exacerbates the issue. To address this, we must deeply understand ourselves, guided by self-love, making mindful choices for our well-being and global harmony. We must address our ignorance by gaining a deep understanding of ourselves, our bodies, minds, emotions, and souls. Self-love is the key to acquiring this knowledge, enabling us to make healthier choices in all aspects of life and solve life's puzzles.

....

According to Vivek Kaushik, a Spiritual Guru and Life Coach, consciousness and the soul are akin to the relationship between the sun and its sunlight. Just as sunlight emanates from the sun and spreads everywhere, consciousness extends throughout the entire body from the soul. In essence, consciousness is the energy of the soul, much like sunlight is the energy of the sun.

If so, all organisms, whether single-celled or multicellular, have a soul because there is no doubt that all organisms are conscious. The difference between human organisms and other organisms is not on a physical, mental, conscious or soul level. Both have a physical body and mind; both are conscious and have a soul. The difference is that human organisms are aware; other organisms aren't. The difficulty is that though humans are aware and intelligent, they are neither entirely aware nor use their intelligence discreetly because their knowledge is half-baked. One well-worn Arab proverb has it that: "nisf al-'ilm akhtaru min al-Jahi – half-baked knowledge is more dangerous than ignorance."   People have been living dangerously for very many decades; because they don't know the reality of their beings. They are not aware of what they indeed are. They don't know who they are, what their bodies are made of, how they function, and where they have come from. In the lack of these facts, they get confused, and their activities mostly end up without direction, causing chaos in their lives and disconnection from their true selves. When you do not know who you are, you cannot utilise your intelligence prudently. When you are confused, you cannot use your intelligence sensibly.

Apart from the human organism, all other organisms do not experience confusion. For instance, in humans, the behaviours of cell organisms are predetermined by their genes. In animals, genes, including reflexes and fixed action patterns, are geared toward ensuring survival, and their innate behaviours aid in this survival. Survival, in this context, means the continuation of life despite danger or hardship. However, the life of human cell organisms is far from simple or easy. They struggle hard to survive because besides getting the food they have to keep their environment free from pollution - toxins. That makes their struggle harder; they work hard round the clock without stopping even for a nanosecond. They cannot survive if the body becomes too toxic; As such, besides loving themselves, they love the environment from where they are best nourished. But for humans, it is not as simple as other organisms; other organisms have to struggle for their physical existence only. But humans have to take care not only of their physical bodies but also their emotional, mental and spiritual bodies, too, because they are intelligent. As such, they need to struggle harder than other organisms. The motivation to work hard comes from recognizing the best work for healthful living physically, emotionally, socially, spiritually, and intellectually! And the best effective way to take care of your whole self – physical and non-physical. When you love yourself you love every aspect of your life. So loving yourself is the panacea for all problems.

Love is the essential ingredient for healing, connecting us to our True Self, which is flawless. Self-love is paramount, allowing us to care for ourselves and share love with others. Self-love means accepting ourselves as we are, with all our imperfections, and having compassion for both our shortcomings and gifts. It involves embracing our unique selves and expressing our true energy. While this true self-love isn't always easy, it's a path to genuine healing and transformation, even if it means facing criticism and ridicule from others.

When someone says, "I love you more than myself," he doesn't know the truth; he doesn't know that he loves or does anything because he exists and can genuinely love others only when he loves himself and his life. If there is no life, there is no love or relation. Self-love paves the way to love others and the world - a universal love. When you love yourself, you connect with your true self on a profound level. Dr. Martin Kettlehurt, in his e-book, encourages you to explore the core of your being, where you can sense the qualities of your true self and your life's purpose. This deep exploration allows you to be open, present, and appreciative of your authentic nature, inviting you to savour and enjoy those inherent qualities within you.

To love yourself is not only a personal solution but also a global one. When you become more self-aware, you also become more aware of your impact on the world. Therefore, sustainability is intertwined with self-love, and improving your own life is the first step toward caring for the planet. Self-love extends to appreciating and caring for the elements that support your existence: Earth, Water, Fire, Air, and Space. These elements provide essential resources and services crucial for your well-being, health, and prosperity. When you care for these elements, you maintain good health and support your body's trillions of cells, which, in turn, sustains a robust immune system and enhances your sensory experiences. Cellular consciousness is at the core of our relationships with ourselves and others, shaping our perceptions and connections with the world.

Maintaining good health is synonymous with self-love. Your body and cells are conscious entities where all experiences happen. Keeping them healthy ensures sharp senses and communication – seeing, listening, smelling, tasting, and feeling – vital for a fulfilling life. Neglecting their care is akin to neglecting yourself, and many illnesses result from this negligence. In our quest for survival, self-care becomes paramount. It's the act of loving ourselves, as the fundamental purpose of life is survival. Living organisms, including humans, require a constant energy supply to sustain life. By prioritising our health, we express self-love and enhance our chances of a healthier, happier existence.

Remember when we took trips to Blue Waters Sirsi Dam Lake? Visits to the home town were incomplete without this.   I am sure, like me, you too felt immediately energetic. You spent all your time in and out, touring about without a stop. We even ate meals whole-heartedly but didn't feel lethargic later. That, my child, is because the quality of the air, water and food in the hills is so much better than our bustling cities. By being a part of a cleaner, greener environment, we ourselves felt much more happy, fulfilled and active.

The essence lies in the five elemental sources of energy: earth, water, air, fire, and space, obtained through relentless effort from the environment. Our lifelong struggles can be in vain without understanding their purpose. Within our bodies, cells teach a vital lesson. These 30-40 trillion cells prioritise self-preservation, safeguarding their existence. Caring for life and its sustenance becomes paramount for survival. Toxins threaten cells and organ function, making pure energy crucial for toxin-free living. Remarkably, cells, though numerous, share a unity of purpose. Unity provides strength; its central goal is a clean environment within your body. This unity extends to your life's interconnectedness, just as cells form tissues, organs, and organ systems. Your environment mirrors this; a clean Earth ensures your well-being. Harmony between self-care and planet care is essential. Safeguarding the environment is our duty, forming the foundation for our planet, communities, and economy. A protected environment sustains ecosystems, benefiting all life. Neglecting protection jeopardises everyone, humans, animals, plants, and more.

In the grand scheme of things, nearly everything in your life, including yourself and the universe, is primarily empty space—99.9999999% of it, as Ali Sundermier's article

"99.9999999% of Your Body Is Empty" reveals. Your body, at its core, comprises atoms that form molecules, the basic chemistry crucial for biology and the world around you. Your body boasts a staggering seven octillion atoms, arranged into vital molecules such as proteins, carbohydrates, lipids, and nucleic acids. These are the building blocks of life, essential for all living beings on Earth, contributing to both structure and function, as outlined in the "Molecules of Life" article on "Basic Biology."

Our bodies, bundles of energy, consist of atoms forming molecules, cells, tissues, organs, and organ systems. Cells, whether in simple organisms like bacteria or complex beings like humans, are life's smallest units, continuously striving for growth fueled by nutrients. Food provides nutrients and toxins, with assimilation occurring in the small intestine, where specialised cells, equipped with tiny projections called microvilli, extract nutrients and transport them into the bloodstream. This process is essential for distributing nutrients throughout the body.

To nourish cells optimally, focus on water-rich live foods like fruits, vegetables, and whole grains. These foods, teeming with essential nutrients, quickly enter the bloodstream, providing pure energy. In contrast, processed foods lack vitality, poisoning cells and causing illness. Most living organisms choose live foods, obtaining pure energy and maintaining health. Humans, primarily consuming dead foods, suffer from diseases, leading to a stressful life. Shifting to live foods can resolve many health issues worldwide, as they promote well-being and can even be grown at home, offering organic and healthy options. Whole grains, soaked or sprouted, are living foods, rich in nutrients, unlike processed grains stripped of vitamins and fibre. Embracing live foods and reducing dead food consumption can lead to a healthier and more peaceful life.

Unfortunately, we are not aware of this truth. And the only way to increase your awareness is self-love. For which you have to know about your body, mind and soul. We are much more powerful than other organisms and the likelihood of success is strong when we work together toward a common purpose. Taking care of our planet, like embracing live foods, is an act of self-love, ensuring our well-being and a harmonious world.

Always remember, my dear,   that one's thoughts are the root of all their actions. These thoughts originate from their mind, which has two aspects: the ego-self and the authentic self. The ego-self tends to focus on financial gains and losses, while the true self engages in win-win thinking. Win-win thinking is the belief that everyone can benefit and succeed together. It promotes abundance and happiness for all parties involved, celebrating the success of others. Embracing this mindset is a path to self-healing. Individuals suffer physically, mentally, and spiritually when they think in terms of advantages and disadvantages. When one thinks win-win, they tap into the cosmic mind or true self, leading to inner peace, automatic healing, and the attainment of disease-free health.

That is what your body is and how it functions. The more you know about it, the more aware and compassionate you will become for your body and everything else in the universe because everything in the universe supports your life. You know now the cause of all suffering in the world is ignorance of the truth. Knowing the truth engenders a solid compulsion for self-love and love for humanity. You want to change yourself and the world. Loving yourself triggers the awakening of your spiritual power, leading to a profound transformation. This inner change holds the key to reshaping the world. Daisaku Ikeda emphasises the potential within all of us to bring forth this transformative power, fostering positive change in any circumstance.

The path to "Love Thyself" involves reconnecting with your true self, cosmic mind, and humanity by recognizing the obscured truth of your being. Understanding life begins with questioning, like "Who am I?" and "How does my body function?" Your body, composed of trillions of cells and atoms, operates from cells to tissues to organs to organ systems. For self-discovery and understanding of life's essence, cultivate self-awareness, love yourself, and your cells, and cherish all that sustains your existence.

Unconditional love is key. Creating self-sustaining global movements requires compassion and inspiring acts of love that lead to healing. Love in action is meaningful; love divorced from action lacks significance. Establishing a supportive environment where individuals assist each other is a powerful way to help ourselves, as Deepak Chopra suggests.

CREATION

"Silence is the language of Creation."- Jane Fuller.

All creations happen in silence. You create a piece of art by going into silence. To conceive an idea of any art form - a painting, a model, a sculpture, a poem, a literary work, an architecture, decorative art, etc. - you have to go into the silence of your consciousness - the source of all creations that turns an idea into reality. As Deepak Chopra states in, "Seven Spiritual Laws of Success" the wellspring of creation is pure consciousness, an untapped potential transitioning from the hidden to the visible. Recognizing our authentic self as a reservoir of pure potentiality aligns us with the force behind the universe's manifestation.

My child, take a moment of calm. You will see hundreds of thoughts and chatters passing through your mind. The chatters slow down when you sit in silence. This too is how meditation starts. Silence is an incubator of creativity where you can nurture your creativity. In silence, you introduce the idea you wish to manifest in reality. It is a bit difficult, but not impossible. It only needs continuity of your silence to keep you absorbed in your creative undertakings. I urge you to practise silence for a few minutes every day.   Practising silence helps you slow or stop the chatter between your silence's recesses for a few moments. There, your idea will start taking form in your consciousness; don't give it a break; practice every day. Slowly your imagination takes shape and order.

Creation unfolds as our thoughts find expression in a fresh form in the physical world. This process can be guided through four steps: (1) concentrating on the problem; (2) observing the ideas that emerge; (3) accepting all ideas, no matter their initial form; and (4) diligently documenting them. The steps are as outlined by Lee Humphries in "How Ideas Shape: The Ecology of Creativity."

Silence is the crucible of worthwhile endeavours. You must embrace silence. Within it, ideas are born quietly, a pleasure unlike any other idea births, like that of a child or a seed sprouting, occur in silence. Beauty emerges quietly but not without the sacrifice of old ideas. As Duane's Dartboard post notes, "Creating something new often requires letting go of something old." Echoing this sentiment, Pablo Picasso said, "Every act of creation is first an act of destruction." Transitions can be painful as they disrupt the status quo, pushing us beyond our comfort zones, especially for those deeply attached to the old ways of doing things.

Excruciating: A mother has to endure nine months to bear a beautiful baby. To be able to become a butterfly, the caterpillar dies. A seed destroys itself to become a tree and then the tree spawns thousands of flowers in silence; flowers destroy themselves to create millions of seeds. The process has the potential to become thousands of forests. No pain, no work of art, and no masterpiece are possible without enduring some pain in silence. No one knows what caused the birth of the universe. There are only theories. The most accepted theory is the theory of the Big Bang, but no one knows for sure, with conviction, what caused the Big Bang. The word "Bang" means sudden loud noise, but It is believed that the Big Bang happened in silence. The Big Bang, despite its name, was a silent explosion—an abrupt release of energy that marked the birth of the Universe, devoid of any sound due to the absence of space to transmit it, as detailed in Maria Popova's article, "The Birth of Sound: Why the Big Bang Was Actually Silent."

Before the Big Bang, Stephen Hawking posits absolute nothingness. Yet, consider a speculation: within this void, a consciousness, the "Cosmic Mother," residing in a minuscule singularity. For aeons, it silently pondered the creation of a flawless universe, birthing it with a beautiful soul and the universal love stemming from the Cosmic Mother's Self-love.

Life is a continuous cycle of creation. Each seed has the potential to spawn countless forests. Deepak Chopra once wisely noted that every seed contains the promise of numerous forests, requiring nurturing. Likewise, your desires are powerful forces, and as Paulo Coelho suggests, the universe conspires to assist you in achieving what you truly want. The birth of a child is a miraculous event. A mother's intense desire attracts millions of sperm, with one eventually uniting with an egg to initiate pregnancy. After nine months of nurturing this idea, a unique and beautiful baby is born. Dianna Mendez, in her article titled "What Makes a Child Special? Ideas for Celebrating Uniqueness," highlights that each child possesses unique strengths and abilities, allowing them to express their individuality. This uniqueness, akin to the inherent characteristics of a seed, defines a child's special nature.

A baby, too, is born unique – one of a kind in the whole universe. What it lacks is the right atmosphere for its nurturing. Instead, it gets confused with the cacophony of voices emanating around. And the people around him make him confused. It needs the proper guidance because, unlike a tree, it is an intelligent but inexperienced being and needs the guidance of coherent people who have the wisdom to help him seek out his unique potential bestowed to his consciousness.

Deep within the tapestry of human existence lies a wellspring of consciousness and potential that accompanies us throughout our journey. The birthplace of true creation begins with knowing oneself honestly. Our ignorance, often veiling this boundless potential, inhibits our ability to express our true selves. To unlock this potentiality, we must embark on a journey of self-discovery, shedding the cloak of ignorance that shrouds our awareness. It is imperative to embrace ourselves fully and to cherish every facet of our being, from the smallest cell to the grandest organ. Much like the harmonious cooperation of cells forming tissues forming organs and organs forming organ systems in a multicellular organism, self-love is the essential ingredient. As Patsie Smith wisely notes in "The Power of Silence: How to Free Yourself from Painful Thoughts," stillness and silence become our allies in this endeavour.

I fervently encourage you to set aside a mere 10 minutes each day, to retreat from the cacophony of daily life. In the embrace of solitude, with closed eyes, let your mind transcend the tumultuous sea of thoughts. The path may seem arduous initially, but persistence is your guide. Do not falter; continue each day. In time, you shall liberate yourself from the shackles of painful thoughts.

Human nature, my dear, presents a duality between the ego and the authentic self. Alas, few are aware of this inner conflict. The ego, as illuminated by Nicole Bayliss in her enlightening article, "The Ego Mind Vs The True Self," is a realm fraught with insecurity, a breeding ground for perpetual misery. In stark contrast, the True Self embodies our authentic essence, forever linked to the cosmic tapestry of "All That Is," resonating with love and abiding by the principle of Win-Win, where cooperation yields gains for all. Yet, if you remain oblivious to your true self, you shall grapple to navigate both your inner realm and the external world. Acknowledge that your ego-self often steers your life, influenced by external narratives that it accepts without question. In contrast, the true self is ever-vigilant, scrutinising the truthfulness of all it encounters.

To live your truth requires honesty with your true self. I must mention Akash Banerjee, a wise soul, founder of Deshbhakt, political satirist, independent journalist, and an Indian YouTuber.

In a candid exchange with comedian Kunal Kamra, he shared two guiding principles: "Never be Dishonest" and "Never be Unfunny." Prioritising your self-perception over the judgments of others is the key to discovering inner peace. Honesty is the path to true happiness, resonating with John O'Donohue's wisdom that honesty leads to feeling at home in your life. Being truthful is a time-saving virtue, as Mark Twain aptly observed, "You don't have to remember anything if you are telling the truth."

In this tapestry of wisdom, my dear, the thread that binds it all together is the profound realisation that knowing oneself honestly is the birthplace of true creation. In the serene embrace of silence and honesty, wondrous creations take root and flourish. Let this truth guide your path, for in its light, you shall find the essence of a fulfilling and purposeful existence.

Unaware, you had that dynamic interaction with your true self as a child. You enjoyed combining your creative thoughts with the creations of the outer world. You had little chance to wander. Reminisce how focused and attentive you were, whether in sports, paintings, writing a poem, dancing around, making up your own code language etc. You were all the time, totally absorbed in your creative space. And, the source of your creative thought is nothing but your true self, often totally disengaged from the outer world. Recalling the moment when illustrating a painting or accomplishing artistry, you made thousands of mistakes. Still, you were never discouraged because you were very close to your own 'creative space' - a creative space where you get the inspiration from within - your inner self. Your mind was focused, attentive, and passionate about perfecting the profile. Muse, how observant and suggestive your inner self was that enabled you to turn all your dreams into reality. It motivated you to discern the minutest detail, and you were entirely absorbed in perfecting every line of your creation. You were allied with your inner self. Your true self convinced you that you could achieve anything you desired. You had a passion for doing things right because you had the freedom and opportunity to brainstorm with yourself, your true self, which never let you down. In his article, Chris says, "You can benefit from interacting with others, but great creative work comes from shutting out the outside world and focusing on your craft." And remember what Picasso said, "Without great solitude, no serious work is possible." That's how you do your best creative work, by tuning out the noise and concentrating on what you do best.

Take Steve Jobs, for instance, the Apple founder. When he was young, he learned something important from his dad while building a fence: "Make the back of the fence as good as the front, even though nobody will see it." He carried this dedication into his work at Apple, where he insisted on perfection in every detail, even the hidden ones. Look at an iPhone's circuit, it's like a work of art. This shows how determination can turn dreams into reality. Steve Jobs changed the world, not just in how we communicate and entertain, but in how we think.

The same longing for precision is intrinsic in you. I know that you made thousands of mistakes, but you have always been determined to turn your creations into a piece of art and make them a masterpiece. Disengaged from the outer world, your inner self encourages you to create a perfect masterpiece; a perfect masterpiece comes from "perfect practice" or total involvement. And total involvement means you are intrinsically motivated, not extrinsically.   Intrinsic motivation, my child, is when you do something because it feels good inside, not for any external rewards or outcomes. It's all about the satisfaction that comes from the activity itself, as explained by Kendra Cherry in her article "What Is Intrinsic Motivation."

Total involvement means the degree of attention, curiosity, interest, and optimism and assigning a reasonable length of time to spend in solitude. Often, passionate people cut themselves off from family and friends and go on a sabbatical for their creative work for a couple of months to complete their creations. Remember that you had that solitude and passion for doing your best. You enjoyed fashioning a new and unique style while creating a model in your fashion school or a piece of fine art. You made your own style befitting in the scheme of things. The quality of your life improves with every passing day. You always tried to create something better than yourself. Unaware, you experienced the richness of your sensory experiences and did all the marvellous things, inspired by your true self and enjoyed every moment of your life. You tried and failed, tested again and failed again. You failed thousands of times, but you were never disheartened. After every failure, you emerge revitalised with a new determination to perfect your work.

As a child, you were very critical and doubted everything because you were honest to your inner consciousness – your true self. A person attuned to their true self is open to their surroundings and pays attention to subtle nuances. You were attuned to subtleties and would not accept anything without evaluating the matter threadbare. The difference of opinion with others was average. You inherently knew that "being different is good". You enjoyed being different from your peers because you looked, felt, learned, and acted differently. You had a revolutionary mind and wouldn't accept anything without arguments. Unaware, you brainstormed with yourself when confronted with challenging issues of importance. This is where you were your most creative self. But after marriage, you missed your playful nature. You become a victim of a belief system. Almost the whole world is a victim of a belief system. The consequences of which are apparent. In my opinion, there is no peace anywhere in the world. There is no security. The problem has become so huge that I see self-aware people desperately looking for a conductive solution.

Still, the super-rich and the governments of the earth haven't yet realised the gravity of this situation. They are busy chasing the mirage of 'development' and are indifferent to the approaching avalanche, thinking their unlimited wealth will help them escape catastrophic situations.

Creating "a thing of beauty is a joy forever". Beauty never fades. The idea of beauty shall not ever fade because it is simply a person's inspiration. But to create beauty you have to rise to higher consciousness. You cannot create a heart-touching poem, a beautiful painting, or any piece of art or writing work without going into solitude; in solitude, you have elevated awareness and elevated awareness is nothing but higher consciousness. In solitude, when you are cut off from the outer world, you experience higher consciousness, the source of all creations. Nothing beautiful can be created without entering your higher consciousness and establishing yourself as your authentic being.

Truth be told, I had no initial idea or thought of writing a book. The genesis of this book was concealed in your letter. My immediate reaction was to reply, not write a book. Your letter concealed the seed of my book which I sowed in my consciousness and energised it with my unceasing loving attention which created the right atmosphere for its growth.

"Silence is the language of Creation."- Jane Fuller.

All creations happen in silence. You create a piece of art by going into silence. To conceive an idea of any art form - a painting, a model, a sculpture, a poem, a literary work, an architecture, decorative art, etc. - you have to go into the silence of your consciousness - the source of all creations that turns an idea into reality. As Deepak Chopra states in, "Seven Spiritual Laws of Success" the wellspring of creation is pure consciousness, an untapped potential transitioning from the hidden to the visible. Recognizing our authentic self as a reservoir of pure potentiality aligns us with the force behind the universe's manifestation.

My child, take a moment of calm. You will see hundreds of thoughts and chatters passing through your mind. The chatters slow down when you sit in silence. This too is how meditation starts. Silence is an incubator of creativity where you can nurture your creativity. In silence, you introduce the idea you wish to manifest in reality. It is a bit difficult, but not impossible. It only needs continuity of your silence to keep you absorbed in your creative undertakings. I urge you to practise silence for a few minutes every day.   Practising silence helps you slow or stop the chatter between your silence's recesses for a few moments. There, your idea will start taking form in your consciousness; don't give it a break; practice every day. Slowly your imagination takes shape and order. Creation unfolds as our thoughts find expression in a fresh form in the physical world. This process can be guided through four steps: (1) concentrating on the problem; (2) observing the ideas that emerge; (3) accepting all ideas, no matter their initial form; and (4) diligently documenting them. The steps are as outlined by Lee Humphries in "How Ideas Shape: The Ecology of Creativity."

Silence is the crucible of worthwhile endeavours. You must embrace silence. Within it, ideas are born quietly, a pleasure unlike any other idea births, like that of a child or a seed sprouting, occur in silence. Beauty emerges quietly but not without the sacrifice of old ideas. As Duane's Dartboard post notes, "Creating something new often requires letting go of something old." Echoing this sentiment, Pablo Picasso said, "Every act of creation is first an act of destruction." Transitions can be painful as they disrupt the status quo, pushing us beyond our comfort zones, especially for those deeply attached to the old ways of doing things.

Excruciating: A mother has to endure nine months to bear a beautiful baby. To be able to become a butterfly, the caterpillar dies. A seed destroys itself to become a tree and then the tree spawns thousands of flowers in silence; flowers destroy themselves to create millions of seeds. The process has the potential to become thousands of forests. No pain, no work of art, and no masterpiece are possible without enduring some pain in silence. No one knows what caused the birth of the universe. There are only theories. The most accepted theory is the theory of the Big Bang, but no one knows for sure, with conviction, what caused the Big Bang. The word "Bang" means sudden loud noise, but It is believed that the Big Bang happened in silence. The Big Bang, despite its name, was a silent explosion—an abrupt release of energy that marked the birth of the Universe, devoid of any sound due to the absence of space to transmit it, as detailed in Maria Popova's article, "The Birth of Sound: Why the Big Bang Was Actually Silent."

Before the Big Bang, Stephen Hawking posits absolute nothingness. Yet, consider a speculation: within this void, a consciousness, the "Cosmic Mother," residing in a minuscule singularity. For aeons, it silently pondered the creation of a flawless universe, birthing it with a beautiful soul and the universal love stemming from the Cosmic Mother's Self-love.

Life is a continuous cycle of creation. Each seed has the potential to spawn countless forests. Deepak Chopra once wisely noted that every seed contains the promise of numerous forests, requiring nurturing. Likewise, your desires are powerful forces, and as Paulo Coelho suggests, the universe conspires to assist you in achieving what you truly want. The birth of a child is a miraculous event. A mother's intense desire attracts millions of sperm, with one eventually uniting with an egg to initiate pregnancy. After nine months of nurturing this idea, a unique and beautiful baby is born. Dianna Mendez, in her article titled "What Makes a Child Special? Ideas for Celebrating Uniqueness," highlights that each child possesses unique strengths and abilities, allowing them to express their individuality. This uniqueness, akin to the inherent characteristics of a seed, defines a child's special nature.

A baby, too, is born unique – one of a kind in the whole universe. What it lacks is the right atmosphere for its nurturing. Instead, it gets confused with the cacophony of voices emanating around. And the people around him make him confused. It needs the proper guidance because, unlike a tree, it is an intelligent but inexperienced being and needs the guidance of coherent people who have the wisdom to help him seek out his unique potential bestowed to his consciousness.

Deep within the tapestry of human existence lies a wellspring of consciousness and potential that accompanies us throughout our journey. The birthplace of true creation begins with knowing oneself honestly. Our ignorance, often veiling this boundless potential, inhibits our ability to express our true selves. To unlock this potentiality, we must embark on a journey of self-discovery, shedding the cloak of ignorance that shrouds our awareness. It is imperative to embrace ourselves fully and to cherish every facet of our being, from the smallest cell to the grandest organ. Much like the harmonious cooperation of cells forming tissues forming organs and organs forming organ systems in a multicellular organism, self-love is the essential ingredient. As Patsie Smith wisely notes in "The Power of Silence: How to Free Yourself from Painful Thoughts," stillness and silence become our allies in this endeavour.

I fervently encourage you to set aside a mere 10 minutes each day, to retreat from the cacophony of daily life. In the embrace of solitude, with closed eyes, let your mind transcend the tumultuous sea of thoughts. The path may seem arduous initially, but persistence is your guide. Do not falter; continue each day. In time, you shall liberate yourself from the shackles of painful thoughts.

Human nature, my dear, presents a duality between the ego and the authentic self. Alas, few are aware of this inner conflict. The ego, as illuminated by Nicole Bayliss in her enlightening article, "The Ego Mind Vs The True Self," is a realm fraught with insecurity, a breeding ground for perpetual misery. In stark contrast, the True Self embodies our authentic essence, forever linked to the cosmic tapestry of "All That Is," resonating with love and abiding by the principle of Win-Win, where cooperation yields gains for all. Yet, if you remain oblivious to your true self, you shall grapple to navigate both your inner realm and the external world. Acknowledge that your ego-self often steers your life, influenced by external narratives that it accepts without question. In contrast, the true self is ever-vigilant, scrutinising the truthfulness of all it encounters.

To live your truth requires honesty with your true self. I must mention Akash Banerjee, a wise soul, founder of Deshbhakt, political satirist, independent journalist, and an Indian YouTuber. In a candid exchange with comedian Kunal Kamra, he shared two guiding principles: "Never be Dishonest" and "Never be Unfunny." Prioritising your self-perception over the judgments of others is the key to discovering inner peace. Honesty is the path to true happiness, resonating with John O'Donohue's wisdom that honesty leads to feeling at home in your life. Being truthful is a time-saving virtue, as Mark Twain aptly observed, "You don't have to remember anything if you are telling the truth."

In this tapestry of wisdom, my dear, the thread that binds it all together is the profound realisation that knowing oneself honestly is the birthplace of true creation. In the serene embrace of silence and honesty, wondrous creations take root and flourish. Let this truth guide your path, for in its light, you shall find the essence of a fulfilling and purposeful existence.

Unaware, you had that dynamic interaction with your true self as a child. You enjoyed combining your creative thoughts with the creations of the outer world. You had little chance to wander. Reminisce how focused and attentive you were, whether in sports, paintings, writing a poem, dancing around, making up your own code language etc. You were all the time, totally absorbed in your creative space. And, the source of your creative thought is nothing but your true self, often totally disengaged from the outer world. Recalling the moment when illustrating a painting or accomplishing artistry, you made thousands of mistakes. Still, you were never discouraged because you were very close to your own 'creative space' - a creative space where you get the inspiration from within - your inner self. Your mind was focused, attentive, and passionate about perfecting the profile. Muse, how observant and suggestive your inner self was that enabled you to turn all your dreams into reality. It motivated you to discern the minutest detail, and you were entirely absorbed in perfecting every line of your creation. You were allied with your inner self. Your true self convinced you that you could achieve anything you desired. You had a passion for doing things right because you had the freedom and opportunity to brainstorm with yourself, your true self, which never let you down. In his article, Chris says, "You can benefit from interacting with others, but great creative work comes from shutting out the outside world and focusing on your craft." And remember what Picasso said, "Without great solitude, no serious work is possible." That's how you do your best creative work, by tuning out the noise and concentrating on what you do best.

Take Steve Jobs, for instance, the Apple founder. When he was young, he learned something important from his dad while building a fence: "Make the back of the fence as good as the front, even though nobody will see it." He carried this dedication into his work at Apple, where he insisted on perfection in every detail, even the hidden ones. Look at an iPhone's circuit, it's like a work of art. This shows how determination can turn dreams into reality. Steve Jobs changed the world, not just in how we communicate and entertain, but in how we think.

The same longing for precision is intrinsic in you. I know that you made thousands of mistakes, but you have always been determined to turn your creations into a piece of art and make them a masterpiece. Disengaged from the outer world, your inner self encourages you to create a perfect masterpiece; a perfect masterpiece comes from "perfect practice" or total involvement. And total involvement means you are intrinsically motivated, not extrinsically.   Intrinsic motivation, my child, is when you do something because it feels good inside, not for any external rewards or outcomes. It's all about the satisfaction that comes from the activity itself, as explained by Kendra Cherry in her article "What Is Intrinsic Motivation."

Total involvement means the degree of attention, curiosity, interest, and optimism and assigning a reasonable length of time to spend in solitude. Often, passionate people cut themselves off from family and friends and go on a sabbatical for their creative work for a couple of months to complete their creations. Remember that you had that solitude and passion for doing your best. You enjoyed fashioning a new and unique style while creating a model in your fashion school or a piece of fine art. You made your own style befitting in the scheme of things. The quality of your life improves with every passing day. You always tried to create something better than yourself. Unaware, you experienced the richness of your sensory experiences and did all the marvellous things, inspired by your true self and enjoyed every moment of your life. You tried and failed, tested again and failed again. You failed thousands of times, but you were never disheartened. After every failure, you emerge revitalised with a new determination to perfect your work.

As a child, you were very critical and doubted everything because you were honest to your inner consciousness – your true self. A person attuned to their true self is open to their surroundings and pays attention to subtle nuances. You were attuned to subtleties and would not accept anything without evaluating the matter threadbare. The difference of opinion with others was average. You inherently knew that "being different is good". You enjoyed being different from your peers because you looked, felt, learned, and acted differently. You had a revolutionary mind and wouldn't accept anything without arguments. Unaware, you brainstormed with yourself when confronted with challenging issues of importance. This is where you were your most creative self. But after marriage, you missed your playful nature. You become a victim of a belief system. Almost the whole world is a victim of a belief system. The consequences of which are apparent. In my opinion, there is no peace anywhere in the world. There is no security. The problem has become so huge that I see self-aware people desperately looking for a conductive solution.

Still, the super-rich and the governments of the earth haven't yet realised the gravity of this situation. They are busy chasing the mirage of 'development' and are indifferent to the approaching avalanche, thinking their unlimited wealth will help them escape catastrophic situations.

Creating "a thing of beauty is a joy forever". Beauty never fades. The idea of beauty shall not ever fade because it is simply a person's inspiration. But to create beauty you have to rise to higher consciousness. You cannot create a heart-touching poem, a beautiful painting, or any piece of art or writing work without going into solitude; in solitude, you have elevated awareness and elevated awareness is nothing but higher consciousness. In solitude, when you are cut off from the outer world, you experience higher consciousness, the source of all creations. Nothing beautiful can be created without entering your higher consciousness and establishing yourself as your authentic being.

Truth be told, I had no initial idea or thought of writing a book. The genesis of this book was concealed in your letter. My immediate reaction was to reply, not write a book. Your letter concealed the seed of my book which I sowed in my consciousness and energised it with my unceasing loving attention which created the right atmosphere for its growth.

CHAPTER NINETEEN

HUMAN POTENCY

Humans have indeed evolved with remarkable cognitive abilities. The power to think deeply and critically is a true marvel of our species. However, as history shows, this extraordinary gift was often underutilised due to blind obedience to authority and belief systems. People followed without question, accepting the words of so-called experts as gospel truth. It was only around 2500 years ago that Socrates, a philosopher of great wisdom, illuminated a fundamental truth. He emphasised that relying solely on those in positions of authority for knowledge and insight is a flawed approach. Power and high status do not guarantee clarity of thought, and individuals in such positions may still grapple with confusion and irrationality. Socrates championed the importance of asking profound questions and engaging in deep thinking before accepting ideas as credible, as discussed in "A Brief History of the Idea of Critical Thinking" in "The Foundation For Critical Thinking."

The habit of obeying authorities has persisted through the ages. Today, it takes a different form, with market forces and the powers that are shaping our beliefs and decisions. These modern authorities have successfully convinced the world that material possessions are essential for success and happiness. They have linked ownership of their products to prosperity, making people believe that hard work is the path to acquiring these possessions. The allure of lucrative job opportunities and venture capital created by the Big Bosses drives people to work tirelessly, inadvertently fueling the economy at breakneck speed. In this relentless and mindless pursuit, individuals have lost touch with their true selves and their critical thinking abilities.

This disconnection from one's true self also results in a loss of human connection, the exchange of positive energy such as love and compassion that sets us apart from other creatures. It disrupts our connection to the information network of the universe, a network vital for the survival of the green surface of our world, of which humans are a part. Nature's well-being is intertwined with ours, and any disruption causes imbalance. The universe's elements work tirelessly to restore harmony without selfishness or judgment, much like the trillions of cells in our bodies that collaborate for our well-being. These cells are quantumly connected to the universal information network, knowing that their existence depends on the health of the body they serve. This intricate web of connections underscores the importance of maintaining our link to our true selves and the broader universe, for in this connection lies the essence of our humanity and the well-being of all life.

The free flow of information is vital for the smooth operation of various systems: celestial bodies, Mother Nature, human bodies, and even organisations. Halting this flow is akin to obstructing the life force. Just as you can't impede your breath or blood circulation without consequences, preventing the free flow of information disrupts the well-being of these systems.

Air and water, essential for nourishing our bodies with oxygen and energy, play a pivotal role in maintaining our health. Any disruption in this delicate balance triggers signals within our minds, manifesting as sensations like hunger, thirst, pain, fever, or nausea. Often, these disruptions are a consequence of unhealthy lifestyles and dietary choices, obstructing the body's natural flow of information. Living amidst pollution only compounds these challenges. This intricate dance of balance mirrors both the cosmos and the workings of the human brain, as eloquently discussed by Andrew Griffin in his article, "The Universe Is Like A Giant Human Brain, Scientist Found."

Yet, in our modern world, the authorities have tirelessly marketed an individualistic and self-centred lifestyle, to a fault where it hinders individuals from connecting with their true selves, nature, and others. The genuine care and compassion we once held for ourselves and our fellow beings have been eroded. This ego-driven mindset, ensnared within belief systems imposed by those in power, disrupts the flow of vital information within us, leading to energy imbalances and a host of ailments. This imbalance lies at the root of all our illnesses, just as a lack of communication can corrode morale within organisations, leading to misunderstandings, conflicts, and mistrust.

The disconnection from their true selves has turned people into mere cogs in the economic machine, driven solely by external forces like market pressures, all in the relentless pursuit of profit. In this dehumanising quest, they have lost the ability to heed the signals emanating from within, forsaking their imagination, reasoning, and emotional connection. The world, once teeming with vibrant human connections, now finds itself ensnared in an emotionless and self-deceptive state.

But if individuals were to awaken from this slumber of self-deception and turn their gaze inward, they would realise the hollowness of many mass-produced products churned out by large corporations. These products often harm human health directly through unsuitable food and medicines and indirectly through massive CO_2 emissions that contribute to global warming and climate change. As the UN's press release poignantly states, climate change is the most significant threat facing humanity today, acting as a "crisis multiplier." It imperils international peace, food security, natural resources, and migration patterns, heightening global tensions. If current trends persist, we risk the collapse of essential pillars of security, including food production, access to clean water, tolerable temperatures, and ocean food chains. The brunt of these consequences will inevitably fall upon the world's most vulnerable populations, underscoring the urgent need for global cooperation and concerted action.

....

The universe, born 13.8 billion years ago, follows a cyclical pattern—birth, life, death, and rebirth. It's believed that the universe's expansion will one day halt, leading to contraction and eventual cessation, be it a big crunch, freeze, rip, or decay. However, there's an intriguing concept of a "big bounce," akin to a cosmic restart, as explained by Lisa Grossman. This notion suggests a cyclical nature, much like the human body's own rhythms. Drawing a parallel between the cosmos and our physical beings reveals remarkable similarities. The universe's distribution of matter mirrors the intricate neural network in the human brain, known as the "connectome," as detailed in TIME. Both the universe and our bodies possess consciousness and a mind. Science journalist Tibi Puiu explores the existence of a "mini-cosmos" within our brains.

Gravity, an omnipresent force, plays a pivotal role in holding cosmic and human bodies together. It shapes celestial bodies, from planets to stars, and orchestrates the tides on Earth, as elucidated in "Gravity: It's What Keeps Us Going." Interestingly, there's a proposed connection between gravity and love. Carrie Lafferty suggests that both can be seen as the cosmic glue binding all things together. Love, particularly, acts as the force interconnecting the universe and everything within it, including our bodies. Self-love, in particular, plays a pivotal role in this cosmic interconnectedness. The human brain, akin to a microcosm, functions in harmony with the universal body, shedding light on the workings of the universe.

When you love your life, that love extends to everything that sustains it. The dynamic force of self-love acts as the adhesive holding the body together. It's this self-love that keeps trillions of cells and the human body united. The cells' sole purpose is survival, and they cherish their existence. To ensure their survival, cells must love their environment—the body—and tirelessly work to keep it free from contaminants. When the body is contaminated, cells suffer. Similarly, when you love yourself, it becomes essential to maintain a pollution-free environment, the source of your nourishment. These nourishing elements are space, earth, water, air, and fire—the same elements that sustain cells. Therefore, nurturing your environment, the wellspring of your nutrients, becomes paramount. The law of universal gravity, akin to the law of love, governs the entire universe. All celestial bodies, from galaxies to stars, the sun, the moon, and beyond, follow this universal law of love. They love themselves and their celestial body—the universe—they are an integral part of.

Deepak Chopra astutely notes that relationships involve a reciprocal exchange, and this principle extends to the relationship between cells and the body. Cells provide essential services to the body and, in return, receive vital nutrients. Chopra's wisdom, drawn from "Seven Spiritual Laws of Success," emphasises that the universe operates through dynamic exchanges where giving and receiving are interconnected. Cells, driven by self-preservation, offer their services to maintain a toxin-free body. Similarly, for your own survival, you must maintain the health of your cells by consuming nourishing food and adopting a healthy lifestyle. Moreover, you must safeguard your environment from pollution since it's the source of your nourishment.

The universal body and the human body possess an inherent capacity for self-healing and self-repair, working ceaselessly. Cells and galaxies alike act altruistically to maintain their body's health because the survival of cells depends on the body's well-being, just as the survival of galaxies hinges on the universal body. This interconnectedness is driven by conscious cosmic energy, uniting the entire universe, including human beings, as a network. The Law of Divine Oneness, articulated by Bre Brown in "The 12 Universal Laws of Manifestation," underscores our interconnectedness through creation by a higher power. This principle transcends the cosmos, impacting all entities, visible or invisible, in the universe, including us. Compassion for ourselves extends towards others, nature, and the universe. This interconnection is the true magic of harmony.

Throughout our lives, we encounter various people, each leaving their unique mark on us. However, only a select few forge a deeply spiritual and lasting connection that resonates within us. This universal spiritual bond underscores the distinctiveness of each individual we meet. Sadly, our lack of self-awareness often leads to indifference in our interactions. Quantum consciousness, as elucidated by James A. Cusumano, PhD, in "Cosmic Consciousness," offers profound insights into achieving well-being, happiness, and success.

Cusumano's experience during Barack Obama's presidential victory speech exemplifies this connection. In his words, "As I listened to Mr. Obama, the camera intermittently scanned the thousands of people in the audience... All of these people look so connected, so much like one."   As he observed the diverse audience, he realised that they all shared an unmistakable sense of unity, despite their differences. This observation aligns with the idea that consciousness is the foundation of existence, as he explains, "Conscious Cosmology maintains that consciousness is the true ground of being." This means that our souls exist beyond the limitations of time and space, and events like Obama's speech have the ability to create a profound sense of oneness among people worldwide.

Cusumano's experience during Obama's speech serves as a powerful example of how consciousness and emotional entanglement connect us all, reminding us of our shared bond as children of the Cosmic Mother. It's a reminder that, as intelligent beings, we have the capacity to recognize and embrace this unity for the betterment of humanity.

The emotions of all of these people have a bond of oneness. Oneness because there is no difference between them on the soul level. There is one soul which is part of everyone. At such contagious moments, everyone feels the same and wants to share their emotions. Emotional contagion involves the spontaneous transmission of emotions and behaviours among individuals or groups. Quantum entanglement, a phenomenon where particles' states are interconnected regardless of distance, exemplifies our enduring emotional connections with all and everything. These connections reflect our bonds with humanity, nature, and the broader cosmic unity we all share. This phenomenon can be well understood if we consider the mother-child relationship. The mother gestated the child in her womb for nine months. What can be a better example of oneness than the oneness of a mother and her child? Mother and child were one when the child was in the womb. Out of the womb, there is a bond of love between a mother and her child. Not only are mother-child related, but the siblings also have a love bond because they have come from the same womb. Distance has no meaning in this relationship. Even if circumstances separate us, with a significant distance, our bond of love never diminishes. In scientific language, this is called quantum entanglement. But I think "emotional entanglement" is more appropriate.   In the larger context, all humans are children of Mother Earth, and they all are related or entangled. We get immediately connected emotionally and want to be a part of suffering or celebration occurring in any part of the world. Our eyes well up in both cases, whether in sorrow or celebration. We experience oneness when we feel sharing a part of the pain or merrymaking.

Everything in the universe is quantumly entangled/emotionally entangled.   All the particles of energy, waves of energy, stars, galaxies, celestial bodies, planets, including our earth and every living or non-living thing you can imagine in the universe are entangled or related because everything is delivered from the womb of Cosmic Mother. Before the Big Bang, everything was one in the womb of the Cosmic Mother. The modern cosmological theory posits that the universe's birth originated from a tiny speck, a singularity, incredibly smaller than an atom, within absolute nothingness. This singularity's explosion, known as the Big Bang, initiated the universe's expansion. Consequently, we can contemplate that all elements in the universe were once unified, intimately connected, and remain so. Cusumano termed this connection "quantum entanglement," which Einstein refers to as "quantum weirdness."

We are intimately and emotionally related and conscious of whatever occurs anywhere in the universe. Though they got physically separated, they still are intimately connected or related or entangled with all the qualities of consciousness. Our heart skips when we learn about solar flares and lunar eclipses. Heart disease deaths have shown a connection with solar storms disrupting Earth's magnetic field, leading to additional cardiovascular-related deaths during high solar activity years, as detailed by Alice Klien in her article "Solar storms may cause up to 5500 heart-related deaths in a given year."

The universe remains intact because of the quantum entanglement or emotional connection among its components, all united in their purpose to prevent disintegration. Like the 30-40 trillion cells in our bodies that work collectively to preserve our health, the elements of the universe labour to prevent its collapse. In this entanglement, time and distance hold no significance, and everything influences each other immediately. Cusumano underscores this with a verse from Francis Thompson's poem, "Thou canst not stir a flower, without troubling a star."

The cause of all troubles in the world is that Humanity has been missing the universal law of oneness. We have forgotten that we are Cosmic Mother's children and have a strong mother-child relationship. We have forgotten that the Cosmic Mother gestated and endured the universe for millions of years before delivering it. Every element in the universe that was delivered from her womb has a mother-child relationship; they all have a purpose to survive and work hard to keep the body of the universe from disintegrating. They know that they won't survive if the body of the universe collapses. After all, humans, too, are the outcome of the same source. Except for humans, no element in the universe has forgotten this relationship. We have forgotten, but it is not lost; it can be retrieved. We only have to jog our memories. And we can be even more efficient because we are aware and intelligent beings. What prevents us from taking the right action is that blinded by our ego mind we aren't utilising our intelligence prudently.

We all, and everything, whether living or non-living beings, atoms, protons, neutrons, electrons, energy particles or energy waves, has come out of the womb of Cosmic Mother. As such, we all are related or entangled. We humans often experience the connection on occasions or events similar to Obama's acceptance speech while watching a happy or sorrowful event taking place anywhere in the world on the TV screen or listening to an emotional speech or description in a book or article, feeling connected emotionally. But soon, we forget and become indifferent. We are indifferent because we are too engaged with the thousands of toys and stories offered to us frequently created by multinational corporations. Our engagement with these toys and stories is so heady and time-consuming that we have missed the essence of life.

Humans missed that relationship. You too, have experienced that feeling of loss. During your moments of solitude, you sometimes find yourself engulfed by that sense of absence, much like an "Empty Hole inside your soul" (quoting Southall Band's "Empty Hole Lyrics"). It's akin to the way a black hole at the centre of the Milky Way pulls in everything that ventures too close. You were bored with the monotony of life and tried to fill it up with meaningless things that give you temporary relief. You couldn't find life's true meaning and essence because you had lost your connection with your soul – your true self. You lost the link and overlooked the nature of reality. Because you don't know who you are, what you are made of, where you have come from, what you want from life and what is your purpose.

Take cognisance of your quantum entanglement, which is no different from spiritual and emotional entanglement. Just as quantum entanglement, spiritual entanglement and emotional relation have no sense of time and space. Love has no boundaries. Inconsequential of time and space, everything happens in the now. The future is happening now in the present, and now is drifting in the eternal past. What goes in the past is stored in your memories. There is no future; there is no past. There is no travel time. Even if you are at the far end of the universe or even on the moon, our emotional connection is immediate without a time lag, just like the quantum connection of a mother with children. We have an emotional connection with Cosmic Mother, Mother Nature with humanity, and everything that occupies our minds. It is a matter of extreme pain that we have lost this connection.

The question that confounds us is when the cosmic brain is perfect, and the human brain is excellent; one can hold the whole universe together; the other can keep the human body organised when there is any irregularity; both can repair and heal themselves, then why is there so much chaos in the world? Why can humans not hold humanity and Mother Earth together they are part of? To find the answer, we need to go back to a few thousand years when people believed that human beings were superior to all other living species and could make or mar the fate of their life or afterlife.

This belief gave rise to a fear of circumstances, a dread of an uncertain future, uncertainties, and risks beyond their control. These fears, in turn, fortified their faith, and the sense of superiority gave birth to egoism. Belief systems sought the guidance of those possessing mystical powers to absolve them of their perceived transgressions. This paved the way for institutions dedicated to gods, overseen by priests and clergy. Initially, these institutions genuinely served the people. Only a handful as such may exist today. Over time, the success of these divine figures led to their arrogance, and they metamorphosed into exploitative institutions, preying on the innocence of the masses. Within these institutions, elaborate narratives were concocted to expand their followership. Devotees contributed to their prosperity through offerings, while the institutions received substantial gifts from businesses in exchange for their blessings. A lucrative industry emerged, propelled by the promise of salvation from hell or the attainment of heaven—a means of manipulating the behaviour of their audience.

Conversely, individuals with immense wealth and overinflated egos pursued riches, power, fame, attention, and validation of their achievements to establish their supremacy. People sought validation from their peers, communities sought approval from other communities, nations sought validation from other nations, and corporations sought global recognition. This quest for validation often manifested as a superiority complex. To sustain this complex, individuals resorted to exerting force, leading to global conflicts and competition among people, communities, nations, and corporations. When governments engaged in conflict, battles and wars erupted, causing widespread destruction. These battles were waged not for a just cause but to assert dominance. Billions of dollars allocated for the welfare of citizens were squandered on weaponry and military research, all in the name of proving heroism while neglecting the pressing needs of their populations. The world possesses ample resources to improve the well-being of its inhabitants, yet these resources are misallocated to research, the accumulation of weapons, and combat. Millions endure extreme poverty while the world grapples with pervasive distrust. Selfishness pervades every corner, and disconnection among individuals breeds destruction on a global scale.

Many have lost touch with their genuine selves, dedicating themselves solely to fulfilling their egos' desires. This has resulted in a decline in genuine values and a burgeoning narcissistic tendency, where individuals excessively rely on external validation. The connection to one's authentic self appears to be waning, supplanted by a fabricated identity. In today's society, the predominant focus revolves around crafting a self-identity centred on material success. The prevailing mantra for prosperity revolves around amassing wealth and financial achievement.

I found more than 4 billion results on a Google search when I queried 'how to make money.' As if the world has no other job but to toil for money. No one seems aware of the world's extraordinarily pathetic and chaotic situation. No one seems aware that the "world is on fire." No one knows that their own house won't be saved if the fire is not doused. They are even unaware that their habit of overconsumption is the cause of the fire. They are not mindful simply because they have lost their connection with their true self. The solution lies in restoring the connection with the true self. But no one seems to know how to restore the connection. A shift in their thinking is needed urgently to correct the anomaly.

CHAPTER TWENTY

THE SHIFT

When we set an intention within the fertile ground of pure potentiality, we harness the boundless organising power of the universe. This conscious transformation relies on two key qualities of consciousness: attention and intention, as elucidated by Deepak Chopra. He states: "Attention energizes, and intention transforms" in his book "Seven Spiritual Laws of Success."

The Cosmic Mother's desire to create a magnificent universe serves as a remarkable example of the power of intention. Her unyielding attention and intense love incubated this idea for millions of years, ultimately resulting in the creation of the universe itself. Just as she manifested the cosmos through her intentions, we, her beloved children, possess the same power to manifest our desires. Grace Denker's words, "The treasure house of the source of all creations is limitless and overflowing," remind us of the abundance within us.

Unlocking this treasure requires us to be honest with our true selves, as Deepak Chopra emphasises. Loving oneself involves accepting every aspect, flaws included. Our true self, as explained by Nagarajan Ramachandran, transcends the ever-changing phenomena of our body and psyche. It's an indivisible essence that animates both, a self-luminous and self-evident truth.

This realisation, though mysterious, signifies a profound shift in consciousness. Just as electricity, though invisible, powers our gadgets, our souls, though unseen, vitalize our being. The mystery lies in not knowing what a soul is and how to harness its frequency. Ignorance about the soul or cosmic mind is the cause of confusion, but loving oneself and knowing oneself, including the mind, body, and soul, can dispel this confusion.

Enter the state of thoughtless awareness, where your full attention is on the present moment, as you create art or engage in various skills. In this state, you receive guidance from your true self, your heart or soul, enabling you to masterfully execute creative endeavours. Thoughtless awareness aligns with Indira Devi's analogy of tranquil water reflecting the true image, allowing clarity in problem-solving.

When your mind is serene, devoid of past or future thoughts, you gain clarity in recognizing problems and their solutions. Consciously managing your thoughts leads to profound self-awareness, empowering you to align your behaviour with your values and accurately perceive others' perceptions of you.

In essence, our capacity for manifestation is intimately connected with our consciousness and self-awareness. We, humans, possess unique cognitive abilities that set us apart from other animals, allowing us to recall and recognize sequential information with precision, as noted by researchers from the City University of New York (CUNY) and Stockholm University.

So, remember the power of manifestation, as it stems from the depths of our consciousness, our love for ourselves, and our unique human attributes. It is a gift we must cherish and utilise wisely on our journey through life.

Only we humans are intelligent and aware. We are aware of ourselves and the world around us. It is just a matter of applying your intelligence more prudently and becoming more aware - aware of your true self and its powers. Isn't it worrying that despite us humans having the gift of intelligence we are not aware of the powers of our true selves? Every human has organising power, and when we become self-aware, we can utilise our organising power more effectively.

Language moulds our reality, endowed with magical potency. Speak to cultivate joy. Your full command of language carries significant influence. Understand that words hold tremendous power, shaping our energy and life's course. Opt for positivity in your speech, as it signals your desires to the universe, enlisting its aid in turning them into reality. You, too, have the magical power to create joy. You, too, can turn your desire into reality – an idea you love to create by giving it your complete attention and saying assiduously your intention with positive words silently into your consciousness. Why do we love an idea and desire its manifestation? Because we want to evolve and progress, just as the universe has been evolving for the last 13.8 billion years and we are part of the universe. The universe is evolving. Humans are also evolving.   Evolution is a slow process, but it can be accelerated considerably faster when we are conscious of its development. "Evolution is a slow process, but it accelerates considerably faster by being conscious of the developments.," - Deepak Chopra. Manifestation of desire accelerates by becoming self-aware and consciously sowing the seed of our desire in the field of consciousness. Our intelligence can think of a plan, organise and manifest it more efficiently when we become self-aware and our intentions are positive and clear. We need to have a firm purpose and determination. The question is what steps we need to take to shift our consciousness from everyday awareness to self-awareness.

"When you truly desire something, the entire universe seems to conspire to aid you." - Paulo Coelho, the renowned author of Alchemist.

Indeed, achieving your aspirations is possible, but it requires more than just desire. You must delve into the purpose behind your wants. Why do you seek these things? It's because you're driven by the fundamental evolutionary needs of survival, growth, and happiness. Yes, happiness has played a pivotal role in our survival by enhancing our adaptability, strengthening our social ties, and increasing our vitality. Individuals who embraced happiness were more prone to pass it down through their genetic inheritance. The cosmic nature of your desires is rooted in your profound consciousness.

A cosmic mind, my dear, is a creative force in motion. Just as the universe continually evolves and expands since its inception, we, too, harbour a desire to create and progress. Evolution, the gradual development of things, is a natural course of existence. What sets human evolution apart is our boundless ambition. Driven by intelligence and self-awareness, we seek to transform our desires into reality swiftly, aspiring to create something superior to ourselves. When we're resolute in this endeavour, it's as if "the entire universe is helping you create it."

Yet, not all ambitions come to fruition, and why is that, you may wonder. The simple truth is that many are not honest with themselves, lacking clarity of purpose. When we are not true to ourselves, our inner joy and freedom become obscured. Self-love is the cornerstone, my dear, but it begins with knowing oneself. Ignorance of our inherent powers leads to confusion, hindering proactive actions essential for manifesting our desires. Proactivity involves making positive changes, preparing, or preventing issues. Highly proactive individuals, according to Stephen R. Covey, consciously choose their behaviour based on values, not conditioning or circumstances.

Humans, unlike animals driven primarily by survival, aspire for more from life. Our unique drive for "more" fuels rapid evolution and conscious development. We possess a conscious cosmic mind, aware of itself and the world around it. This awareness compels us to seek change, to create our universe. However, we often fall into a reactive mode, waiting for external responses before taking action. This occurs because we are not entirely honest with our true selves, our cosmic minds. The root of this dishonesty lies in ignorance. Removing this ignorance is the key to transforming our desires into reality.

Self-love, my dear, is paramount. It is not contingent on external affection. The deepest love emanates from within, encompassing the well-being of our body, mind, and soul. Embracing self-love, as emphasised by Akansha Narang in her article "How Self-Love Makes You More Attractive," enhances our self-perception and attractiveness to others. Self-love is the catalyst that not only transforms us but also our desires. By infusing our intentions with loving attention within our consciousness, we make our desires alluring.

Just as a seed needs the right conditions to grow into a tree, our desires require the fertile soil of our consciousness and the nurturing light of loving attention. Transformation commences with this loving attention, and it stems from self-love.

"Every act of creation is first an act of destruction," as the saying goes. To become a tree, the seed must destroy itself. A caterpillar must undergo a transformation to become a butterfly. Similarly, we must dismantle our ego-self to turn our desires into reality. Meditation, my dear, encourages the release of the ego, forging a profound connection to the universe. This practice dissolves the sense of separateness, eliminating fears and desires tied to the self. It opens the door to embracing all aspects of existence.

Letting go of the ego initiates a shift in our consciousness, elevating us to a higher state of awareness. In this elevated state, we tap into our limitless capacity for organisation and creativity. We can destroy our ego-self by spending a few minutes each day in solitude or meditation. In doing so, we plant the seed of our desire within our consciousness, giving birth to our ideas, dreams, and desires, and watching them flourish.

There should be clarity of your desire and determination to achieve no matter what comes your way. You are prepared to go through trials, tribulations, and risks. You will wait for its manifestation before putting in any other desire. Your mind is infused with that desire and has a passion for that; failures won't deter you. Most of all, you must have a purpose, and the purpose is to seek goodness for yourself, your cells, humankind and everything that supports your well-being. You will meditate on your dream desire for a few minutes every day in silence. Focus your attention and silently affirm your desire, akin to planting a seed in the boundless field of Infinite Organizing Power, as suggested by Deepak Chopra. Your intense desire resonates through your cells and the universe, both eager to manifest it. The universe operates as a vast interconnected family, spiritually and quantumly linked, attuned to your desires. However, complications arise when your desires lack clarity and focus, hindering your mind's effectiveness.   When you have a sharp focus your mind connects with everything in the universe. Every element of the universe becomes restless to turn your desire into reality. Because all elements, whether matter or non-matters, are conscious and are quantumly connected, with everything else. You are connected with everything, yourself, humanity, Mother Nature, and the entire universe. Your desire is conveyed immediately to everyone.

In our exploration of the power of manifestation, we must first recognize that the universe comprises three fundamental substances: dark energy, dark matter, and normal matter. These elements, intriguingly, are quantumly entangled. Everything visible to our eyes falls under the category of normal matter, composed of energy particles known as atoms. It encompasses the entirety of the cosmos, from stars and galaxies to celestial bodies, planets, and even ourselves—human beings and all living and nonliving entities. All of this is an integral part of the universe. Your mind, consciousness, and soul are not separate from this grand cosmic tapestry. When you plant the seed of your desire within your consciousness, the entire universe conspires harmoniously to manifest your passions into tangible reality.

Now, it's crucial to understand that all forms of matter are essentially condensed energy. The intriguing question arises: how did this energy condense into matter? Although we lack a definitive answer to this profound inquiry, one thing remains clear—consciousness pervades every corner of the universe. While we can't ascertain the existence of entities in the universe that think like humans and possess the intent to create their desires, the omnipresence of consciousness in the cosmos cannot be dismissed. Let's entertain the notion that such conscious entities may exist, akin to humans in their intentions and their ability to focus attention, which, in turn, leads to the condensation of energy particles into matter. This idea may be speculative, but it serves as a reasoned contemplation. After all, it aligns with how humans harness their intentions to manifest their desires into reality.

In this context, the power of manifestation is intrinsically linked to the interconnectedness of the universe and the presence of consciousness within it. Whether it's the seed of a desire sown in your consciousness or the focused intention of a conscious entity in the cosmos, the fundamental principle remains the same—the universe conspires to bring forth that which is intended. It is a testament to the remarkable potential and power that we, as conscious beings, possess to shape our reality.

So, as you explore the depths of manifestation, remember that you are not separate from the universe but an integral part of it. Your desires, when nurtured with intention and attention, can indeed become a tangible part of this cosmic dance, where energy transforms into matter, and dreams manifest into reality.

....

In her article, Genevieve Gerard discusses how, according to the teachings of the Ageless Wisdom, the soul is not only an inherent part of one's essential nature but also a potent resource for personal transformation. Human transformation, as described by Allaya Cooks-Campbell in her article, entails an internal shift that aligns individuals with their highest potential. This transformation influences every facet of life, shaping one's perception of the world and their role within it. The soul represents the highest energy within people. By embracing soul consciousness, individuals can align with their utmost potential, driven by their innate intelligence.

The primary barrier to this alignment is ignorance. Many are so occupied with the demands of daily life that they lose touch with their souls. Life becomes routine, and it may seem that nothing will ever change. This happens due to over-involvement and a lack of time to contemplate the nature of the soul and its incredible capacity. The idea that they possess the power to align with their highest potential through their soul often doesn't cross their minds.

Dhaval Gala's book, "Know Your Soul," defines the soul as the self, the inner "I" residing within the body, guiding its actions. Without the soul, the body is like a mobile phone without a SIM card, a light bulb without electricity, a computer without its CPU, or a robot without its programmed software. Essentially, the soul not only powers life but also imparts meaning, purpose, and identity to everything.

Consider this: people breathe with the assistance of their souls, and even as they read these words, it's their souls that enable understanding. When they make a mistake and feel the need for correction, it is their souls that recognize the error and suggest improvements. The soul constantly provides help. What's missing is the conscious awareness that the soul is assisting. It aids them hundreds of times daily through their senses, intuition, and instincts. Their subconscious minds are at work, guided by the soul, even if they aren't consciously aware of it. Imagine the incredible potential when one consciously harnesses the power of their soul.

The soul operates like a finely tuned algorithm, intricately programmed with a specific purpose, which is the overarching mission of one's life. However, many may not be fully conscious of this purpose. Deepak Chopra emphasises that life's purpose revolves around the conscious recognition of one's true self, an essence that is boundless and ever-present. It centres primarily on one's essence rather than their actions. When career, beliefs, and behaviours align with one's inner being, they can evolve while the life purpose remains constant. By living in the present moment and utilising unique talents to serve others, individuals naturally fulfil their soul's mission. Once they recognize their true selves, their souls, they can fully tap into their incredible power.

You used your soul all through your academic career because then you loved yourself and enjoyed doing things you loved. Then you were free to explore the world on your own. Unwittingly you were your genuine self and were comfortable acting your true self. Unfortunately, you didn't know that you were acting your true self. Post your academic career you were faced with the real world. You started caring more about other people's lives, likes, dislikes, interests, and everything, but you never try to know what your true self is and what is the call of your soul. You missed your connection with your true self. For decades you have been missing it but have not the slightest idea of the cause of your missingness and often felt a void in your life. You wrongly tried hard to make enough money to fill the void. Whereas your purpose is about your being or your existence and finding joy in life through purpose. And the only way to fulfil that purpose is love - love with self and everything that supports your life.

Loving yourself is akin to embracing the power of manifestation. When people truly love themselves, they align with the essence of existence itself, for their existence is intertwined with the grand tapestry of the universe. This connection, my dear, is the key to unlocking the extraordinary power of manifestation.

When individuals shower themselves with self-love, they grant their desires the precious gift of attention. Just as a flower captivates us with its purity, this attention renders their desires alluring. It's the purity of intent that lies within, stemming from their true, unadulterated self.

In this journey of compassionate self-love, there's a profound intertwining of emotions – respect, trust, and affection. Such love is not selfish; it extends beyond the boundaries of the self. When people want something with a compassionate heart, their desires are transformed into magnetic forces that draw the universe's assistance.

You see when one loves their true self with compassion, they place an unwavering trust in the vast cosmos. In return, the universe feels obliged to conspire in their favour, assisting them in achieving their heart's desires. This symbiotic relationship between self-love, compassionate wants, and the universe's support is the very essence of the power of manifestation, my child.

PUSHING THE ENVELOPE

"The point of being human is to push the envelope of being human."- Deepak Chopra.

The terms "human being" and "being human" may seem similar, but they have distinct meanings. In the article "Difference Between Human Being and Being Human," Hasa explains the difference. "Human being" refers to a member of the Homo sapiens race, while "being human" denotes displaying unique human qualities. Our innate kindness, generosity, and ambition are ingrained in human beings. Research suggests that genetics play a role in our kindness. We're born to be compassionate and driven. Ambition, defined as the desire and determination for success, is a natural trait. Many see being born ambitious as a positive trait, characterised by a relentless pursuit of goals. Motivation, essential to fuel ambitions, can be intrinsic or extrinsic. Intrinsic motivation arises from personal satisfaction, driven by one's interest or enjoyment in a task. It's not influenced by external factors or societal pressures. You are born with these qualities, and motivation can come from within, driven by your personal satisfaction and interests.

Here lies the crux of the matter. You are not aware of two kinds of motivation. Suppose you do not know the difference between intrinsic and extrinsic motivation. Your default option is usually extrinsic motivation. Intrinsic motivation is vital, as external motivation can have adverse effects. The pursuit of external rewards like money, praise, or power may undermine intrinsic motivation. Intrinsic motivation originates within, driven by personal enjoyment and satisfaction. Extrinsic motivation, on the other hand, comes from external rewards. Being true to your authentic self means embracing intrinsic motivation, doing things because you genuinely enjoy them and find personal satisfaction.

You "chase good things" in life when you are intrinsically motivated.   You remained true to yourself during your childhood and academic life. Though you were not conscious of the two sources of motivation, you naturally chased good things in life because you were naturally intrinsically motivated. Then you were not affected by the external world, and you remained true to your authentic self during that time. And naturally, you pushed the envelope for being human. But sometime after finishing educational time, some cataclysmic change sneaked into your life unwittingly. You had no idea how the change occurred, but it was calamitous. Slowly but surely, you got disconnected from your true authentic self, your intrinsic self.

In the realm of self-love and care, lies the key to igniting your inner drive. External motivations, they're like a tempest, disrupting the gentle dialogue within. Your body, a wise compass, is ever ready to guide you toward the right path.

In an article where Claire M Fletcher-Flinn delves into Matthew Blakeway's work, "The Logic of Self-Destruction," the concept takes shape that our minds function as intricate biological computers, following a precise set of action algorithms. Blakeway raises profound doubts about the reliability of these algorithms, especially when they're founded on faulty data and moulded by our beliefs. He underscores the fact that emotions and beliefs, elusive as they are, can't be directly perceived; they're deduced from our actions. Blakeway posits that humans are inherently inclined to construct environments that bolster survival by pursuing positive emotional outcomes and evading unfavourable ones. It's a drive deeply rooted in our biology, but it can lead us to be ensnared within belief systems, where we unreservedly accept input from unseen influences like society and the market.

In essence, as we drift away from our "biological algorithm," akin to a recipe for our conduct, we also drift from our authentic selves. Our actions become mirrors of what the market forces desire from us. In this disconnection, we inadvertently commit acts of blindness, following market forces without questioning their intent, driven by a desire to fill the emptiness within. This emptiness stems from the illusion of lacking something vital. The remedy lies in dispelling this illusion and embracing the truth. Understand that you lack nothing; you are whole and complete. It's a truth hidden within, often overshadowed by ignorance. You are unaware that kindness is woven into your very genes, that your wholeness and completeness remain obscured. To dispel this ignorance, reconnect with your true self and shower yourself with love.

The silver lining, dear one, is that although you've drifted from your biological compass and authentic self, the connection remains stored deep within your subconscious mind. And the finest key to unlocking it is self-love. Self-love opens the gateway to your subconscious mind, a treasure trove of your true essence. As Kimberly Friedmutter enlightens us, this subconscious realm, hidden beneath our conscious awareness, cradles our emotions, memories, instincts, and survival mechanisms. It possesses an infinite memory capacity, never forgetting a thing, holding a boundless wellspring of ideas. All it takes is to bridge it to your conscious mind, a bridge built with compassionate self-love. Loving yourself means cherishing your life. To love your life is to love yourself and all that sustains it. Your cells and your surroundings, nurture your existence, much as each cell loves itself and the environment that cradles it – your body. Love, you see, is an intrinsic element of creation, intricately woven into the fabric of the universe. While the brain moulds our tangible experience of love, its deepest wellspring lies within the soul.

Always bear in mind, that everything gains life and meaning through your presence. When you harbour compassion for yourself and the world around you, everything conspires to nurture your existence. Love your own being, adore the trillions of cells that comprise your body. Love your mind, your emotions, your soul. Love the environment that cradles your life. Love the five elements that sustain you each moment. Life, dear one, is no zero-sum game; it's a symphony of interconnectedness. To find happiness, you must also sow the seed of happiness in others. When you cradle your baby with love, both find joy – a mutual triumph.

Cultivate gratitude for all that supports your life, for gratitude often ignites virtuous actions. When we recognize the kindness of others, it stirs within us the urge to reciprocate. Understand that everything, every facet of existence, supports and aids us. This realisation is the path to reclaiming our humanity, to reconnecting with our authentic selves, and to embrace our humanity in full. To be human means perpetually pushing the boundaries of our humanity.

CHAPTER TWENTY-TWO

A GIFT OF LOVE

"Nothing can be created without love." Creation ex nihilo means that divine love is the sole force behind everything's existence. It signifies that everything emerged from love. (Source: Created out of nothing means created out of love by The Christian Century)

When there was nothing, love was the driving force. The Cosmic Mother's love birthed a magnificent and flawless universe with celestial bodies like suns, moons, stars, planets, and galaxies, including our own planet Earth. What's most remarkable among her creations is the emergence of a self-aware, conscious, and loving cosmic mind in humans. An incredible unique gift of love because the human mind has the same intelligence as the Cosmic Mother. Humans have the same capacity to create anything they desire out of nothing. The difference is that the human/individual mind is confused because it has many levels of consciousness. The distinction between the individual mind and the Cosmic Mind lies in their states. The individual mind is often deluded and conditioned, burdened with judgments and confusion.

However, through dedicated mindfulness practice, surrender, and devotion to the Universal Self, as explained by Suddhaanandaa Brahmachari in "Turning Into The Cosmic Mind," the individual mind can gradually shed its conditioning and return to its innate purity, aligning with the Cosmos, the Self, or the Soul.

This book you are holding in your hand, too, is a creation of love; It was created out of nothing. The seed was positive thinking. Your thoughts wield immense power in shaping your world and reality. To take control of your destiny, mastering your imagination and thoughts is crucial. When you steer your thoughts and imagination effectively, you draw the things you desire and wish to experience into your life, as explained in "How Thoughts Create the World and Reality."

I had no idea of writing a book. My immediate reaction was to reply to your letter, not write a book. I failed and was frustrated.

I looked for ways to accomplish the task and then the idea of writing a book struck my mind. Your letter concealed the seed of my book which I sowed in my consciousness and energised it with my unceasing loving attention which created the right atmosphere for its growth.   You raised some disturbing questions in your letter, and I was humbled.

It stirred a strong emotion of love for you and a desire to do something to compensate you. I started replying but was abashed and felt perturbed by not finding the right words to express my deep love. Perhaps it was my pure, unconditional love for you that made me want to write a perfect reply, and I found it impossible to inscribe in a few pages. I had never entertained the idea or thought of writing a book. But as I reflect on my life, I hope to share a piece of my mind and soul with you. There was not even the slimmest idea of book writing. But somewhere deep within dormant was a hunger to impart my life's experiences to you. Your letter aroused my long-held desire. I saw an opportunity to open my heart and realised after a while that I had to write a book to communicate the lessons I learned from my life.

That was the moment the seed of the book sowed in my consciousness. Which was energised by my unceasing loving attention. I wanted to give you all the lessons I learned in my life.

I wanted to show you how much I love you. Your letter awakened my latent love and desire to communicate life's lessons to you. I had limitless pangs of remorse and love, which gave birth to this book - it is a creation of love. You can see the tremor of love for yourself - the cause of my inspiration to write this book. It was love for you two that helped me fashion this book. I meditated and meditated and meditated to create the right atmosphere for the seed to blossom. The entire universe conspired to support turning my desire into reality from the womb of nothingness. Now it has become a large tree. I hope not only you but humanity has a chance to savour its fruit.

You too are bestowed with this gift. But you are not yet aware of this incredible gift of your cosmic mind. Unaware, you have been carrying this miraculous gift for a long time, unexplored. "There are two great days in a person's life - the day we are born, and the day we discover why."- Mark Twain.

Discovering the immense power of cosmic energy is a momentous revelation. Latha emphasises, "Love is the Cosmic Energy...the Energy of Life." This book is my heartfelt gift to both of you and all those close to your hearts, including your family on Earth. In truth, all of us, as humans, are children of the Cosmic Mother – Mother Earth – even though physical distances may separate us. As Latha beautifully puts it, "The separate self does not exist – Our souls are mirrors of each other's souls," much like how Obama's acceptance speech united millions worldwide, transcending the constraints of distance. Distance became inconsequential. I hope that this book will aid you in discovering your boundless cosmic potential, and your cosmic mind and that it will inspire anyone who reads it.

I am ending this book with a heavy heart feeling and a tribute to the great poet Jalal ad-Din Muhammad Rumi, a Persian poet and Sufi master born in 1207, whose poem "A GIFT TO BRING YOU."

inspired me greatly. I take the liberty to reproduce his poem here, which is worth many volumes of books:

"You have no idea how hard I've looked for a gift to bring You. Nothing seemed right. What's the point of bringing gold to the gold mine or water to the ocean. Everything I came up with was like taking spices to the Orient. It's no good giving my heart and my soul because you already have these. So I've brought you a mirror. Look at yourself and remember me."

I hope my book will prove a mirror to help you see your genuine persona and free you from all conditions.

End

www.ingramcontent.com/pod-product-compliance
Lightning Source LLC
Chambersburg PA
CBHW040750120726
48005CB00012B/1131